Adult Literacy Policy and Practice

DOI: 10.1057/9781137535115.0001

Other Palgrave Pivot titles

Brendan Howe: Democratic Governance in Northeast Asia: A Human-Centred Approach to Evaluating Democracy

Evie Kendal: Equal Opportunity and the Case for State Sponsored Ectogenesis

Joseph Watras: Philosophies of Environmental Education and Democracy: Harris, Dewey, and Bateson on Human Freedoms in Nature

Christos Kourtelis: The Political Economy of Euro-Mediterranean Relations: European Neighbourhood Policy in North Africa

Liz Montegary and Melissa Autumn White (*editors*): Mobile Desires: The Politics and Erotics of Mobility Justice

Anna Larsson and Sanja Magdalenić: Sociology in Sweden: A History

Philip Whitehead: Reconceptualising the Moral Economy of Criminal Justice: A New Perspective

Robert Kerr: How Postmodernism Explains Football and Football Explains Postmodernism : The Billy Clyde Conundrum

Ilan Bijaoui: The Open Incubator Model : Entrepreneurship, Open Innovation, and Economic Development in the Periphery

Pilar Melero: Mythological Constructs of Mexican Femininity

Rafael Kandiyoti: Powering Europe : Russia, Ukraine, and the Energy Squeeze

Cristina Sánchez-Conejero: Sex and Ethics in Spanish Cinema

Matthew Gritter: The Policy and Politics of Food Stamps and SNAP

Bridget Kevane: The Dynamics of Jewish Latino Relationships: Hope and Caution

Nataly Z. Chesky and Mark R. Wolfmeyer: Philosophy of STEM Education: A Critical Investigation

Seung Ho Park, Gerardo R. Ungson, and Andrew Cosgrove: Scaling the Tail: Managing Profitable Growth in Emerging Markets

David Michalski: The Dialectic of Taste: On the Rise and Fall of Tuscanization and other Crises in the Aesthetic Economy

Adam Okulicz-Kozaryn: Happiness and Place: Why Life is Better Outside of the City

Palash Kamruzzaman: Dollarisation of Poverty: Rethinking Poverty Beyond 2015

John A. Mathews and Hao Tan: China's Renewable Energy Revolution

palgrave▶**pivot**

Adult Literacy Policy and Practice: From Intrinsic Values to Instrumentalism

Gordon Ade-Ojo
University of Greenwich, UK

and

Vicky Duckworth
Edge Hill University, UK

DOI: 10.1057/9781137535115.0001

First published 2015 by
PALGRAVE MACMILLAN

Palgrave Macmillan in the UK is an imprint of Macmillan Publishers Limited, registered in England, company number 785998, of Houndmills, Basingstoke, Hampshire RG21 6XS.

Palgrave Macmillan in the US is a division of St Martin's Press LLC, 175 Fifth Avenue, New York, NY 10010.

Palgrave Macmillan is the global academic imprint of the above companies and has companies and representatives throughout the world.

Palgrave® and Macmillan® are registered trademarks in the United States, the United Kingdom, Europe and other countries.

ISBN: 978–1–137–53512–2 EPUB
ISBN: 978–1–137–53511–5 PDF
ISBN: 978–1–137–53510–8 Hardback

A catalogue record for this book is available from the British Library.

A catalog record for this book is available from the Library of Congress.

www.palgrave.com/pivot

DOI: 10.1057/9781137535115

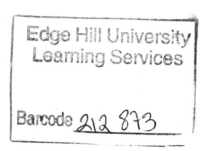

Contents

DOI: 10.1057/9781137535115.0001

palgrave▸**pivot**

www.palgrave.com/pivot

1

Exploring the Concepts: Instrumentalism, Philosophy of Education, Ideology and Value Positions

Abstract: *This chapter critically engages with the philosophical drivers of education and considers how they inform and shape educational polices and specifically adult literacy. Value positions are explored through the prism of two broad educational philosophical constructs of instrumentalism and libertarianism. We relate this to ideas and debates within these areas for current issues in educational policy and practice. In specific terms, such libertarian values as intuitionism are held as counterpoint to the various strands of rationalist value in education.*

Keywords: adult literacy; ideology; instrumentalism; libertarianism; philosophy; policy

Ade-Ojo, Gordon and Vicky Duckworth. *Adult Literacy Policy and Practice: From Intrinsic Values to Instrumentalism.* Basingstoke: Palgrave Macmillan, 2015. DOI: 10.1057/9781137535115.0002.

Introduction

The semantic core of the title of this book is focused on the concept of instrumentalisation. It is apt, therefore, that our preliminary task must be to explore the nature of the term instrumentalisation. However, this is not an exercise in finding the literal meaning of the term. Rather, it is more a question of locating it in the appropriate context within the discourse of educational policy. In order to adequately engage with this initial task, we shall make two comments for the purpose of clarification. First, the term instrumentalisation must be seen as a derivative of the more basic term, instrumentalism. Second, in the context of this book, instrumentalisation is in itself a mere process. In other words, we see the term as reflective of a process within a movement and as such, our main focus would be to simply locate the process within the framework of a larger movement.

As with many such engagements, our natural instinct is to head for a dictionary to find the meaning of the term. While general dictionary definitions are frequently shown to have their limitations particularly in terms of locating terms within the relevant context, there is no doubt that dictionary definitions often have their own merit. Not least, because they at least offer us a non-complex view of the semantic denotation of the words under investigation. In essence, they offer us a starting point in our excursion into the semantic field enveloping the relevant term.

One simple definition of the term instrumentalism is offered in the WordSense.eu dictionary (online – we are in an era of digital learning after all):

> A pragmatic philosophical approach which regards an activity (such as science, law or education) chiefly as an instrument or tool for some practical purpose rather than in more absolute or ideal terms. (WordSense.eu, 2015)

Along a similar line of reasoning, the *Encyclopaedia Britannica* offers us a definition by Neufville (2014) as:

> The view that the value of scientific concepts and theories is determined not by whether they are literally true or correspond to reality in some sense…is the view that scientific theories should be thought of primarily as tools for solving practical problems rather than as meaningful descriptions of the natural world.

From these two initial excursions into the meaning of instrumentalism, two issues emerge. The first is the fact that instrumentalism is a process borne out of a particular perception. Instrumentalism as a process, therefore, can only emerge, for those who hold a particular perception

DOI: 10.1057/9781137535115.0002

of what the process means. The second issue is the fact that both defi-nitions have clearly located the concept of instrumentalism within the framework of a larger realm: philosophical positions. The two issues are, of course, related: in order for the former to materialise, there must be an engagement with the latter. Developing a perception that informs a process is a by-product of engaging with a philosophical position.

In the context of the ongoing, we suggest that a more fruitful engage-ment would be to explore the larger realm, philosophical positions, if we are to understand the contextual import of the term instrumentalism. Furthermore, as a significant part of this book will be looking at various philosophical perceptions including instrumentalism, we conclude that it is best not to dwell too long on exploring the term in isolation here. Nonetheless, we shall offer a preliminary description of the term which draws from the two 'simple' definitions cited earlier.

In the first instance, we suggest that instrumentalism is seen as a position encapsulated in the phrase 'a means to an end'. In order words, it is a position that symbolises that which is not intrinsic. That is, the value is not inherent but extended to another source or outlet. Second, instrumentalism is a philosophical concept which will naturally induce a range of 'what is?' questions. In essence, instrumentalism is best seen as a philosophical position that can be applied to various areas/disciplines including education, which is our focus in this book. In the end, it is apparent that we cannot talk of instrumentalism without recourse to the larger concept and context of philosophical values. That is what we shall now turn our attention to.

Philosophy of education

Now, we approach the more complex question of 'what is?' We, however delimit our focus to the realm of education, as that is our concern in this book. From the onset, we acknowledge the onerous nature of answering 'what is?' questions. Phillips (2013) provides an insight into the complex nature of finding answers to 'what is?' questions. While exploring the nature of philosophy of education, Phillips notes that:

> What is ...? Questions are extremely troublesome, in large measures because it is rarely clear what answer would satisfy the questioner' and that, 'it is virtually certain that the first answer that is received – and very possibly the latter ones as well – will be unsatisfactory. (p.3)

DOI: 10.1057/9781137535115.0002

Attempts by various authors have demonstrated this complexity. Not the least, because most authors have tended to approach this question by focusing upon key terms and their cognates. Indeed, various attempts at engaging with the concept have tended to display a form of atavistic tendency. At the root of what we consider atavism in this context is the predisposition to interrogate cognate terms and in doing this, to explore what philosophers do and where they do it.

There are ample illustrations of this form of engagement with the task of attempting to unravel the phrase, philosophy of education. In his interesting contribution to Bailey's (2011) edited book *The Philosophy of Education*, Standish (2011) starts with a framework which he then attempts to fill by providing answers to various questions including what do philosophers do? What is philosophy? What sort of reading might philosophy of education entail, and what is education? From the amalgam of answers to these questions, he crafts out what remains a 'non-defined' description of the phrase. By his own admission, what he has done 'falls short of providing a definitive account of the philosophy of education' (p.9). In essence, therefore, this difficulty in carving out a definitive account of such terms as the philosophy of education might well be because 'most important concepts are essentially contestable' (p.9). Other authors have taken a similar approach and, not surprisingly, have come to the same conclusion (see, e.g., Barrow, 2013; Maxwell, 2014).

In our view, a major reason for this seeming impasse in providing a definitive account of the term is the fact that authors have frequently engaged with the cognate terms philosophy and philosopher, and then sought to build upon these in defining or perhaps describing 'philosophy of education'. A necessary fallout of this approach is often the limitation of our understanding of the nature of philosophy of education. This frequently used approach focuses on philosophy as the source of explanation and indeed, the definition of the concept, as if philosophy of education were an end in itself and has no relationship to or bearing on other activities. Philosophy of education, then, from this perspective, is focused on the activity and has the tendency to ignore the impact of such an activity on an ultimate product which might manifest in different sociological realms.[1]

We suggest, however, that answering such a question need not be so complicated. The pivot of this approach, in our view, lies in the fact that the ultimate outcome of such an engagement is the provision of answers that are geared towards the one who raises the question 'what is the

DOI: 10.1057/9781137535115.0002

philosophy of education?' In other words, the answer is solely induced by the questioner. For us, however, the goal must not, and should not, be induced solely by the dictate of the 'questioner'. Rather, the 'answerer' must also set out clearly the intended message. Drawing from semantic principles, the ultimate communicative act must draw on a convergence between the speaker and the hearer, and in this context, the 'questioner and the answerer'. It is the latter viewpoint that informs the approach that we take in this book in initiating our answer to the question: what is philosophy of education?; what have we used the term to mean? Nonetheless, the complexity involved in providing an answer to the question, what is philosophy of education, remains implicit.

In order to fully illustrate both the complexity and the outcome of engaging with a definition of philosophy of education using the approach which we have earlier highlighted , we shall present a summary of the product of such an engagement by one author. From the onset, we must emphasise that there is nothing particularly significant about the work we have chosen. As far as we are concerned, the choice is informed by the fact that it is able to illustrate our argument and provide evidence of the complexity involved in defining the term, as well as offer us the opportunity to introduce our own dimensions to the process of defining the term.

Probing a philosophy of education

Our chosen illustration is the chapter written by Phillips (2013, pp.5–18) in the *Sage Handbook of Philosophy of Education* (2013) edited by Bailey, Barrow, Carr and McCarthy. As reflected in the title of this chapter, the concern is 'philosophy of education'. Phillips starts by acknowledging what is perhaps accepted by most people who have worked in this area – the complexity of the term. Almost predictably, Phillips' approach is to identify three dimensions through which the task of defining the philosophy of education can be approached. This immediately sets out two major issues for consideration: what philosophy of education is not and the complexity involved in defining it. In respect of the latter, he notes that his approach might well provide a 'slow, complex and indirect answer to the apparently simple question: what is philosophy of education' (p.4). But by just noting the extent to which debates have popped up at every turning in our brief engagement with this term, we

DOI: 10.1057/9781137535115.0002

are convinced that most readers will agree that defining this term is anything but simple.

In clarifying what the term is not, or ought not to be, he draws a distinction between two usages of the word philosophy. On the one hand is the vapid non-technical usage of the word philosophy which has a dictionary definition as 'what anyone who thinks abstractly' (p.4) does. Aside from the fact that this tells us little, the non-decisive nature of this entry suggests that children are more of philosophers than anyone else. As far as we know, children are quite capable of thinking abstractly, particularly with regard to how they engage with and construct their own language use. On the other hand is the use of the word philosophy to refer to the 'work done in university departments of philosophy or programmes in philosophy of education'. While this, at least, offers clarity on where philosophy is done/carried out, it still neither tells us what this work is nor how it is done. Again, this little input deepens the complexity involved in defining the term.

Another seemingly simplistic definition emerging from the approach of looking at cognate terms is 'philosophy is what philosophers do' (p.5). But we assume that every reader will by now be asking the question, who is the philosopher? Phillips himself acknowledges this, plays around with a potential definition of philosopher as 'anyone who thinks deeply', but in the end, discards it because of the unlimited boundaries it is capable of crossing.

Having discarded these seemingly simplistic definitions, Phillips sticks to the goal of defining the term philosophy of education by mapping out three things. Who engages in it, what does that engagement involve and in which domain does the engagement take place? He draws on three existing seminal works to illustrate the three and thus sets out his own definition of the term. In essence, he uses philosophical principles elicited from specifically chosen input by three scholars to elucidate his perception and argues that there are different constructs of the philosopher, different types of work they engage in, but fails to clarify whether all of this can, and does happen, in only one domain.

The first of these contributions is the constructivist theory of learning (Curren, 2007; Glaserfeld, 1995, 2007). At the heart of this theory is the view that 'knowledge is not found or discovered, but is made or constructed by humans' (Phillips, 2013, p.7). For now, we shall only look at Phillips' disquiet about some areas of this theory. First, he registers a sense of unease in respect of the potential for insularity that this theory

DOI: 10.1057/9781137535115.0002

projects. How, he asks, can we be sure that the knowledge internally constructed by individuals is not simply relevant or peculiar to the individual, and will, therefore, not reflect a universal position? Second, he highlights the potential contestation of issues around the replication of knowledge: How can we be sure that 'the knowledge I have constructed is identical with, or compatible with, the knowledge you have constructed' (p.7). In essence, the theory has not really addressed the realistic potential for multiplicity of knowledge in which everyone has the right to claim that their own 'knowledge' is valid and true as against others' knowledge. This, of course, underscores the potential tension inherent in the possibility that the learner's knowledge can be divergent from the teacher's knowledge. In Phillips' view: the natural confusion emanating from the two issues identified earlier and the emergence of a whole range of modern interpretations of constructivism has inevitably led to some form of confusion which demands the intervention of analytic philosophers. A product of such an analytic engagement has resulted in the following:

1   Construction of knowledge by individuals is from the materials being learned and not simply from some boundless data source. It is the essence of what has been labelled the 'individual psychology' dimension of constructionism (Phillips, 2000, 2007).
2   There is a public discipline focus of constructivism which acknowledges individual contribution to already publicly available 'knowledges' in various fields.

Developing from these different realms of constructivism, the individual versus the social construction of knowledge as exemplified by the differences in the arguments of Piaget and Vygotsky, respectively, it becomes evident that there is the need to modify the often generalised description and claims of constructivism as a learning theory. Who, we might ask, takes responsibility for this work on discerning the specific from the general? We shall, of course, return to this theory as a means of highlighting the ways in which Phillips has attempted to answer the initial set of questions we raised: who, what and where?

The second piece of work to which Phillips anchors his search for a definition is Skinner's engagement with the explanation of human action in which he explored the differences between behaviour and state of mind. Having established his hostility towards the principles of metaphysics, Skinner clearly sets out his rationales for the logical positivist

DOI: 10.1057/9781137535115.0002

position which sees observation and or behavioural perceptions as the heart and soul of experimental studies. He then applies this position to the study of human behaviour, and in his view, this moves such a science from the unseen to the 'see-able' (see Skinner, 1972).

Drawing from Skinner's work as explained briefly above, Phillips offers a central conclusion: Skinner's work cuts across disciplinary boundaries and has, therefore, 'had a pronounced impact on educational practice' (Phillips, 2013, p.10). Given that Skinner himself was not essentially an educationalist but a psychologist, the key point developing from his work was, in Phillips' view, the fact that many elements of his work are to be found in the work of many educational researchers. Clearly, Skinner's work is applicable, not only across disciplines, but also across periods. We shall return to the significance of this within the framework of Phillips' definition at a later stage.

The third theoretical work to which Phillips' exploration is anchored is Rousseau's educational philosophy as embodied in his narrative on *Emile*. The central thesis of Rousseau's theory is that when a child is 'unencumbered by the forces of civilized society, his natural tendencies are allowed to express themselves' (Phillips, 2013, p.11). Expatiating on this argument, Rousseau wrote: 'harmony becomes impossible. Forced to combat either nature or society, you must make your choice … you cannot train both' (1955, p.7). In other words, learners are torn between their natural dispositions and societal expectations. If we gave room to the pull of the latter, there are likely to be conflicts which might not be easily resolved. In contrast, if we gave room to the former, the synergy between the learner's nature and what they intend to learn is likely to smooth the path of learning. Rousseau himself underscores this inherent conflict by painting in very bold relief the contrast between Emile's education and a sketch of that of Sophy, Emile's soulmate. He encapsulates Sophy's education in the following words: ' [i]t follows that woman is specially made for man's delight … she ought to make herself pleasing in his eyes and not to provoke his anger; her strength is in her charms' (p.322). Although there will undoubtedly be justifiably strong views about his sketch of Sophy's education, those views are not the concern of this phase in this work. What is important is the emergence of what Rousseau saw as a guiding principle that should inform education. There is no doubt that many advocates of radical educational reform in Western Societies have drawn from these principles. It is very evident that some of the ideas of Dewey and indeed those that were the underpinning drivers of the

DOI: 10.1057/9781137535115.0002

famous British 'free school' Summerhill resonate with Rousseau's principles (Phillips, 2013). What is clear from this, then, is the fact that some scholars are involved in a particular type of work that ultimately leads to the generation of ideas and principles which have lasting significance in terms of informing the shape of the arguments that will subsequently emerge in their field of work.

What use does Phillips intend to make of the role and nature of these three theoretical contributions, we may ask? How do they contribute to his definition of the concept of philosophy and the work that philosophers do? The first conclusion he draws is that there are different conceptions of philosophy and the way each manifests itself can be related to the three summarised theoretical case studies .

Drawing from case study 2, the Skinnerian behaviourist argument, Phillips suggests that there is an object-level as against meta-level engagement with theory. Like the authors of this book, Skinner had no direct link with philosophy as a subject. Yet, his contribution was such that he provided a set of guidelines for those who are interested in studying behavioural patterns, regardless of the field in which they work. Object-level, therefore, can be seen as that level of engagement which draws from, and focuses on, a particular subject area. In contrast, the meta-level of work is that which is not particularly concerned with subject area knowledge but which produces principles that have wider applicability. In Phillips' (2013) words, it is a kind of endeavour that 'gazes down at level one [object-level] discourse between practitioners' (p.13). Skinner's work, in this context, therefore, epitomises a particular conception of philosophy which engages with the production of general principles across disciplinary divides.

An initial description that we can, therefore, carve out for the work done by philosophers might be, that it is not necessarily about knowledge in a particular area, but about how 'knowledges' can be welded together under a principle or principles. Hence, philosophers are not necessarily subject specialists. Having said this, it is clear that philosophers who engage in object-level work can move in either direction. That is, they can both engage with their specific subject area and a wider scope of coverage. Enough about Skinner and his relevance to Phillips' definitions for now, as we shall subsequently revisit this in order to draw out the implication for our own perception of the work philosophers do.

Developing upon this classification of the scope of the work done by philosophers, Phillips then attempts to provide his own classification.

DOI: 10.1057/9781137535115.0002

He draws from Frankena (1969) in identifying what he calls the three concerns of philosophy. According to him, these are concerned with:

1 man's position relative to the universe;
2 providing guide to action through the formation of goals, norms and standards; and
3 enquiry and criticism.

One remark about this classification: just from browsing through the curriculum of most philosophy departments in higher institutions, we may conclude that the focus of philosophical studies, and indeed, the dominant discourse in this discipline are the first and third concerns identified by Phillips. Yet, concern 2 is also crucial. A focus on concerns 1 and 3 suggests that this is the work that can only be, and is usually, carried out in higher education institutions. We note here that this is not essentially true. Indeed, the concern of this book is to locate the effect of the work done by philosophers outside of institutions. This brings into focus the twin issues of the domain in which the work of philosophers is done and the applicability of their product.

A simple semantic analysis of Phillips' three concerns suggests, as does Phillips himself, that the first concern is majorly an exercise in speculative endeavours. The second can be seen as normative or prescriptive, while the third is purely analytical. In order to clarify the relevance of this categorisation, we return to Phillips' case studies. The normative concern of philosophy is likened to Rousseau's *Emile*. In *Emile*, Rousseau offers what he considers the best way to educate young people (albeit of the male species) and offers guidelines on the way in which their education must be constructed and what it must contain. Similarly, Skinner, though focusing on how to conduct scientific investigations, provides guidelines that must be followed. For him, this originates from the analysis of logical positivism and concludes that in the study of humans and animals, the only focus must be on the observables. The work of constructivists is equally relevant in this context. They suggest that the best way to facilitate learning is by providing the space for learners to construct their own knowledge. Again, this is another guideline that is offered as the only, or at least, the best way to facilitate learning. The result is that educators who buy into the constructivists' ideas continue to advocate for the development of, and adherence to, pedagogies that empower learners. Navigating through the various stops within the frameworks of these theories, Phillips finally appears to have arrived at

DOI: 10.1057/9781137535115.0002

his final stop. But what then does philosophy of education mean? We can extrapolate a number of features that provide a form of definition through the answers provided to our original who, what and where questions.

First, in respect of the question what, the product can be seen as a set of guiding principles, descriptions and pronouncements on the state of being that can either sit within a subject area or discipline, cut across disciplines or focus on issues other than just subject knowledge within a discipline. In respect of the question where, it would seem that this endeavour is seen in general terms as consigned to the rarefied world of academia. Following these, the answer to the question who is implied in the answer to the second question. The location, we may assume, is again in academic organisations/institutions.

Philosophical work, in the context of Phillips' engagement, can thus be described as involving that type of work done in order to provide guiding principles and explanations at different levels and in different areas, that explain and or dictate how the concerns of such areas are to be carried out. To transfer this to the specifics of philosophy of education, we borrow Phillips' (2013) own dictionary-type definition: 'Philosophy of education is a field where philosophical inquiry is pursued that focuses upon issues arising within the domain of education' (p.18).

We are in no doubt that this definition will perhaps leave the reader not any more enlightened about what philosophy of education is than when we first engaged with Phillips' journey. Nonetheless, there are obvious foundations upon which one might build. We, therefore, seek to build upon this foundation as follows.

In the first instance, Phillips' definition of 'what' appears to be ambiguous. What sort of inquiry takes place in the field of philosophy? Just drawing from Rousseau's views in *Emile*, which represents Phillips' account of analytic and normative concern of philosophy, it is clear that the focus can be twofold. On the one hand, it engages with providing guiding principles on what ought to be, while on the other hand, it explores what is. These two dimensions represent the normative and analytical dimensions of the product of philosophy of education.

Second, we revisit the issue of the domain in which the work of philosophy is done. Phillips' engagement gives an impression that this work is done mainly within institutions such as universities. We, however, seek to take this further. If the work is done within and limited to academic institutions, one gets the impression that the product is an end in itself.

DOI: 10.1057/9781137535115.0002

As we have suggested earlier, such a view will, in the first instance, exclude the present writers from engaging with this work. Although we work in academic institutions, we are not philosophers by any stretch of imagination. Yet, we believe that we have legitimate grounds for engaging with this type of work because the implications of the product of people conventionally labelled philosophers extend to our own field of work. In this context, we again echo Phillips' concept of meta-level work. On the basis of this, we suggest that though the domain of philosophy of education might have its base in academic institutions, it goes much wider and includes areas such as policymaking. In order words, the product of philosophical inquiry might well be seen as guidelines or principles that inform decision making at different levels and in different contexts. The key for us here is the applicability of the product of philosophical enquiry. In his contemporary society and subsequently, Rousseau's principles, as embodied in *Emile*, became the driver of educational policy guidelines at various points. Hence, we add to Phillips' view; philosophy of education provides guidelines which impacts on other areas of endeavour and is, therefore, not an end in itself, but a means to an end. It is in this context that we are currently engaging with this debate. Guiding principles from various schools of thought have, in our view, informed different policy positions in adult literacy. Our concern in this book, therefore, is centrally analytical, although we expect to also have elements of the normative. Indeed, Sayer (2011) makes a related point:

> The most important questions people tend to face in their everyday lives are normative ones of what is good or bad about what is happening, including how others are treating them, and of how to act, and what to do for the best. The presence of this concern may be evident in fleeting encounters, and mundane conversations, in feelings about how things are going, as well as in momentous decisions.

Having established that there is an additional dimension to the work that philosophers do in terms of the domain of impact, it becomes inevitable that we further modify the view about those engaged in this work. If a particular group of philosophers produced guiding principles on the best content for the education of young people, that piece of work, it might be argued, is of no pragmatic importance unless those who make policy on the education of young people buy into it and utilise it in their policymaking. It follows, therefore, that such policymakers cannot be excluded from the group of those who engage with the production of educational

DOI: 10.1057/9781137535115.0002

philosophy. At the very least, they constitute the outlet for testing these ideas and principles. As such, the work done in this area is not limited in any way to the domain of academics. As a preliminary conclusion, therefore, we recognise the validity of Phillips' definition, but explicitly extend the domain and the product to include such practical realms as policymaking in particular. It is this that is central to this book.

Leading on to the next section then, there are two key issues that we now need to address. First, what are the areas of education in which philosophical guidelines are utilised, and second, how does the relationship between philosophy of education and policy work?

Philosophy and policymaking in education

One of the few consensuses to emerge from the previous section is the agreement that one of the main products of any engagement with philosophy is the generation of guiding principles. We also argued that such principles are not to be seen as ends in themselves, but as means to various ends. Indeed, those principles are to be utilised in other contexts and ultimately yield another level of guidelines. Rousseau's philosophy of education, for example, has been utilised by educationists and policymakers to generate a set of guidelines for teaching practitioners. Hence, there are levels and stages to the utilisation of the products of philosophical inquiry. In the context of educational policy, which is our main concern in this book, how does the first level of philosophical product relate to the next level?

For us, a useful way of setting out this relationship is, ironically, by looking at the relationship between the two terms that are sometimes used synonymously: philosophy of education and ideology in education. How do these two differ? When the current Tory government in the United Kingdom opted to cut public spending and consequently shrink public services, one of the more frequent comments was that such cuts, or indeed policies leading to cuts, have been ideologically driven. In the same breath, many commentators have referred to a Tory philosophy which is seen as informing these policies.[2] In essence, these two terms are sometimes used interchangeably. For us, however, there is a difference between the two, and by understanding what this difference might be, we are likely to better understand how a philosophy of education might relate to policymaking in any particular field.

DOI: 10.1057/9781137535115.0002

Before attempting to draw out the differences between the two, let us see what the literature has to offer in terms of defining each of them. A typical definition of philosophy is offered in Standish (2011), who suggests that philosophy of education involves 'exploring how we think [about education] and the ideas lying behind our thinking' (p.7). In essence, the concern of philosophy of education is located in the abstract realm and simply does not involve doing experiments or collecting any form of empirical data. Yet, philosophers are keen to align their ideas to the notion of truth. The implication here is that the product in this context is often located in a form of logical truth which constitutes the evidence base for philosophers.

Ideology, on the other hand, refers to a set of beliefs and doctrines that back a certain social institution or a particular organisation. Unlike philosophy, which refers to looking at life in a pragmatic manner and attempting to understand the principles behind why life is as it is, ideology expresses dissatisfaction with the current state and aspires to some future state. Philosophy tries to understand the world in its current state. Therefore, put simply, ideology is aimed at changing the world whereas philosophy is aimed at seeking the truth about it. It is in the context of the fixation of ideology with changing the status quo that the two differ in essence. More importantly, it is within the context of this difference that the relationship between philosophy of education and policymaking emerges, as we shall attempt to show in the section that follows.

An interesting insight from one blog (Ingrid@bloggerroundtable, 2015) suggests, rightly in our view, that ideologies depend a lot on philosophy. It argues that each and every ideological approach is based on some underlying philosophical truths. The converse, however, is not considered to be true. Philosophy does not have underlying ideologies. Thus, it is understood that while philosophy can be independent of ideology, ideology is dependent on philosophy.

For us, an ideology of education is a by-product of one or more philosophies of education. An ideology is the form in which philosophy engages with policymaking. When philosophies are generated, they are anchored to some form of logical truth and, therefore, usually open to debates. However, when politicians who engage with policymaking buy into a particular philosophy, more often than not, they generate ideologies from these philosophies and insist that these are sacrosanct. Ideologies, therefore, constantly have an impact on the society, whereas philosophy does not have such a direct impact on the society. Ideology

DOI: 10.1057/9781137535115.0002

aims at spreading beliefs. It also aims at imposing those beliefs on the members of the society too, whereas philosophy aims to explain society as it is and offer guidelines on how best to engage with it.

Drawing from the ongoing, we hope that it is becoming fairly obvious that there is a substantial difference between a philosophy and an ideology. Although it is true that a philosophy generally informs the direction of our political engagement, that does not preclude an engagement in discussions and arguments. Philosophies remain dependent on and open to evidence of new learning and to critical discussions of their applicability. The end result, therefore, might actually be a principled consensus, or indeed, an agreement with the principles embedded in a different philosophy.

In contrast, with ideology, a decision has already been made about what is best for society. In simple terms, a policy has already been developed based on a philosophical position. As suggested by Ingrid@ bloggerroundtable (2015), 'You know all the answers, and that makes evidence irrelevant and argument a waste of time, so you tend to govern by assertion and attack.' Ideologies, therefore, bring answers from philosophy to the table of policymaking. Blattberg (2015) encapsulates the basic differences between a philosophy and an ideology and sets out the ways in which each one relates to governance. For him,

> Political philosophies are distinguished by their different conceptions of political dialogue. Being philosophies, they are obviously going to be very general such conceptions, although they differ as to how general they conceive themselves to be: some claim to be abstract and to have universal relevance while others are affirmed as more relative to context. Either way, conceptions of the form that political dialogue does and ought to take will be connected, implicitly or explicitly, to positions regarding other philosophical matters, such as the nature of the interlocutors as well as of the medium of their speech, that is, language. (p.1)

In essence, while engaging with philosophies, although we may anticipate discussions on overarching principles or maxims, there is relatively little to say about specific issues. Setting out how this differs from ideology, Blattberg notes,

> Political ideologies, by contrast, being much more programmatic than political philosophies, are concerned with little else. Instead of general accounts of the form and content of political dialogue (although ideologies always assume these, even if only implicitly), ideologists are more interested in guiding us as regards the positions that we should take on particular issues. So they will

DOI: 10.1057/9781137535115.0002

make proposals about the kinds of things that we ought to be saying during actual dialogues. (p.1)

He concludes: 'Ideology, then, is the stuff of political culture, of law, institutional design, and policymaking'. We add, philosophy is the stuff of intellectual engagement. Now, let us use two conflicting economic philosophies and their attendant ideologies to illustrate the relationship between the three: philosophy, ideology and policymaking.

In our view, a lot of the social problems that have confronted, and are still confronting the United Kingdom are informed by a fastidious adherence to specific ideologies that are informed by different philosophical positions by succeeding governments. The result is that a vast majority of the decisions taken by succeeding governments are informed by advice from ideologically driven people. The immediate past government was consumed by the Keynesian economic philosophy which might be surmised as; the wealth and resources of the state are safer when under the control of the state rather than individuals. The ideology emanating from this philosophical position has led ideologues within the policy-making instrument of the state to insist that government manipulation through monetary policy actions, hands-on fiscal legislation, heavy taxation to support state projects and a heavily regulated private sector were the best policies to adopt for the progress of the nation. These are, of course, products of ideological fastidiousness. As a result, there was a massive expansion of the state sector, a huge outlay on public facilities and, of course, a massive debt. Without being political, we think it is safe to agree that the New Labour government did not leave the country in the best shape.

That, however, should not detract from the fact that their Keynesian outlook benefitted the country in the areas of education, health and welfare. The crucial question for us is: how much better would they have done if they had been guided by the flexibility offered by philosophy rather than the rigidity of ideology? If they had listened to rational philosophical discourse and agreed that it is possible that other areas of governance such as trade and the economy, employment and other related factors could have been better administered through a recourse to the arguments of the Smithian economic philosophy?

On the other hand, the current government subscribes to the Smithian economic philosophy which puts forward the argument that wealth creation must be located in the hands of individuals within the state. The ideology fashioned out of this philosophical position will not budge on

DOI: 10.1057/9781137535115.0002

the perception of how the country must be run. The ideologues within the government insist on a similar pattern of single-minded ideological allegiance, fuelled by academics who are followers of Adam Smith's theory. They insist on the invisible hand of the private sector rather than governmental intervention, a limit to the role of the state and the creation of private wealth. Economists are often positioned to discuss the merit or otherwise of either of these models. However, from a broader lens as stated by Dorling (2015, p.389), 'people on the left and right construct their stories, testaments and beliefs as to the way to behave'. Obviously, proponents of the two ideologies remain at counterpoint on this issue. One of the crucial questions to be resolved remains: is wealth accumulation about survival or greed?

Let us be plain here. Drawing on our experiences as practitioners, activists and academics we strongly suggest that some of the current policies, particularly in spheres other than the economic are ideologically driven. Indeed, our honest view is that a flexible approach which an economic philosophy could have offered might admit the possibility that other viewpoints could be effective in different spheres and might well offer desired solutions. In the contemporary setting, ideology has exerted so much influence on policymaking that, education, welfare and health have all been consigned to the postulations of the Smithian theory. It is early days yet after an election that has returned the government to power, but the rumblings of unease and disaffection seem to suggest that there may be trouble ahead.[3]

From these discussions, the message we hope would have emerged for our reader is simple: Philosophies (and, therefore, a philosophy of education) breed ideologies which in turn could be directly responsible for the form and shape of policy. Policies, therefore, have an indirect relationship with and to philosophy. That relationship is often mediated by policymakers who are politicians or members of a particular class, who insist that their chosen policy direction is supreme.

Having established this, let us now turn to the literature to see how the definitions of ideology converge with our sense of reasoning discussed and might, therefore, shed further light on what the philosophy of education might connote. Small (2005) introduces another dimension to our understanding of ideology. Drawing from his analysis of the Marxist theory of ideology, he identifies an element of what might be classified as falsehood in the essence of ideology. He notes: 'Ideology is a system of false beliefs which, it is assumed[,] are imposed by some ruling class on a

DOI: 10.1057/9781137535115.0002

dominated class' (p.74). For us, this becomes very relevant in the context of policymaking. Policymakers in this context represent the ruling class, while the dominated class represents civil society. More importantly, the source of the so-called false belief is more often than not a philosophical framework into which the ruling class and/or policymakers in this case, have bought. Marx himself digs deeper in his analysis on this when he talks of what he calls 'phenomenal forms' which masquerades as current forms of thought. In essence, while we can see the latter as philosophical positions, ideologies are manifested in the former. We return, therefore, to our earlier description of the relationship between ideology and philosophy of education. Philosophy of education in this sense can be seen as current thoughts on education in its various spheres, while ideology in education can be seen as the personalised interpretations given to these thoughts by different groups depending on their personal experiences.

Gee (2015) in his engagement with ideology and literacy sheds further light on the difference between the two terms by exploring the history of the word ideology. While acknowledging Marx's notion of false consciousness, he cites Napoleon's rejection of the Enlightenment Philosophers and his subsequent substitution of their argument with what Gee calls 'knowledge of the human heart' (p.9). This encapsulates the difference between the two. While the philosophy of education will offer guidelines backed by evidence and logical argument, ideology will simply introduce the personal human dimension to the interpretation of the arguments of a philosophical position.

In our view, it is the latter that policymakers are often predisposed to adopt. Having said this, it remains a valid argument to state that one draws from the other. As illustrated in the Napoleonic example presented earlier, the Enlightenment Philosophers had backed their social theory with evidence. In his rejection of their position, however, Napoleon, as a man in pursuit of power and a policymaker, did not offer a different or rival theory. Rather he provided a different interpretation of the same philosophical position by claiming 'to be in a position to know the knowledge of the human heart and the lessons of history better than others' (Gee, 2015, p.9), and in so doing, 'privileges his own experience over the claims to knowledge' (p.9) coming from any other interpretation of this philosophical position. Within the framework of the two contributions explored, our hope is that the relationship between ideology and philosophy on the one hand and how that relationship informs policymaking on, the other hand, becomes more explicit.

DOI: 10.1057/9781137535115.0002

Educational foci of philosophy

As with any other sphere of human endeavour, education has a huge coverage with many aspects to it. In recognition of this, we cannot merely assume that any engagement with the philosophy of education will cover every aspect in the same way. Indeed, those who work in the area of philosophy of education recognise that different spheres of education are covered by different philosophical positions or arguments although there can be a common underpinning principle to all of them. For example, in his exploration of a philosophy of education, although recognising the different spheres of interest, Marx associates his philosophy to the principle of the concept of social reproduction. As such, he argues that with education, we have to 'consider, therefore, several more or less distinct kinds of ideology in education' (Small, 2005, p.78). On the basis of this, he identifies three foci of philosophical work in the field of education: a philosophy that is built around society itself which involves arguments about what is taught and learned; ideologies built around what is commonly termed 'the hidden curriculum'; and a third which is built around the experience of school. While this classification is not particularly central here, it gives an insight into the varied contexts in which work in the area of philosophy of education can be carried out and indeed offers a wider sociological lens.

In a much simpler and less political analysis, Bailey (2011) argues that it is important to deconstruct the scope and coverage of philosophy of education studies because by doing so, research into the area 'tends to develop better if a narrower and more focused topic is selected' and also because 'there can be more to say about something quite specific and limited than about the meaning of life' (p.12). In pursuit of the 'better development' that such a narrowness of focus suggested by Bailey might offer, we suggest that a sound starting point would be to look at the potential areas that work in this area might focus on. We, therefore, offer a summary of classifications in the section that follows, including the contributions of Bailey (2011) that hold the same view.

Philosophy of education can involve engaging with questions of conceptual clarification. In this context, the primary focus would be to explore themes and concepts that are prevalent in the policy and practice of education. It would in effect involve an in-depth analysis of policies in education and more importantly tease out the underpinning drivers/ philosophies.

DOI: 10.1057/9781137535115.0002

Another focus would involve engaging with the issue of values. In this context, such an endeavour would tease out various positions on the rationales for making particular decisions or for taking particular actions. Issues around the nature of knowledge, social justice, thinkers and their positions on educational issues, critique of policy positions and a potential combination of any of the identified foci (Bailey, 2011) could also be the focus of an engagement with the philosophy of education.

For us, however, merely listing these aspects is not an end in itself. As we have highlighted earlier in this chapter (see p.10), it is important to be aware that outputs of an engagement with philosophy can be normative, analytical, enquiry-based/critical. The classification of the various foci of work in the field of philosophy merely highlights the fact that engaging with different aspects of the philosophy of education can yield different outputs. For example, it is reasonable to expect that an engagement with the issues of conceptual clarification and values is most likely to yield an analytical product. Then again, engaging with issues relating to decisions about what best to include in a curriculum and the best policies for education might likely belong to the realm of normative outputs which prescribes a perceived best way of doing certain things. More importantly and from the point of view of the focus of this book, it is the engagement which generates normative outputs that policymakers are most likely to involve themselves with. In essence, the extension of the domain of the work done by philosophers to areas such as policymaking is sure to be informed by the philosophical focus of the work and the output it is likely to generate. Policymakers, therefore, are less likely to be concerned with a purely analytic output. Rather, they are more likely to be interested in a field that facilitates the generation of normative outputs.

In consideration of this, it is important to clarify that our focus in this book is on both normative and analytical outputs of philosophy of education. In the subsequent two chapters, we explore the nature of policy in adult literacy and seek to explore philosophical explanations which would appear to have been seized upon by policymakers, in order to generate what might ultimately be considered as ideologies rather than philosophies. In the latter part of the book, we offer an alternative valued position arguing that this position will be more beneficial to all in the field of adult literacy. In furtherance of that course, we provide a form of normative guidance on what is good and what is bad.

DOI: 10.1057/9781137535115.0002

Educational value positions: what we ought to teach

As we have argued earlier, normative work in philosophy of education would usually generate outputs that seek to provide guidance on what ought to be in various spheres in education. Such outputs often materialise as value positions in the philosophy of education discourse. As a result, there are several treatises on what we ought to include in the curriculum and what we ought to consider a worthwhile educational enterprise, and so on. In this section, we look at the outputs in respect of one of the spheres, the content of the curriculum. Central to this are the key questions about what we ought to teach and the values that we associate with education. Drawing from our understanding that the main goal of education is 'to change people in some way', values in this context must involve 'judgements about what changes are desired' (Degenhardt, 1982, p.7). Two main foci of contention emerge here: who ought to make the judgement about what ought to be taught and what ought to be learnt?

With regard to these questions, a crucial issue is that of neutrality. Could sound but neutral judgements be made about what people ought to be taught and about what people ought to learn regardless of who makes these judgements? There are two remarks we would like to make in this connexion. First, this brings into relevance the issue of ideology as against philosophy. If judgements were made or informed by ideological convictions, which we agreed might be a product of 'false consciousness', we could be in danger of imposing false values. Second, it is clear that our appreciation of the merit of any value position will vary depending on the viewpoint from which we look at these value positions. Hence, the value position acknowledged as having merit by a policymaker, who has to consider various factors outside of education, might be considered totally worthless by an individual who is only concerned about his/her own progress. Similarly, the merit associated with different value positions is likely to vary depending on the ideological inclinations of whoever is involved in the evaluation of these value positions. So, we can be sure from the onset that there is no one answer or one incontestable truth where the issue of value positions and their adequacy is concerned.

There are several value positions offered in the literature and this leads to serious confusion for two reasons. First, it becomes difficult

DOI: 10.1057/9781137535115.0002

to distinguish between several terminology used by different contributors and second, it is difficult to understand who exactly these values are meant to inform or influence. In response to this we propose two frameworks for the analysis of value positions in education. In proposing these frameworks, we make no claims about their invincibility, but merely suggest that they are viable as instruments for analysis and for easier understanding of how value positions might inform patterns in other areas.

We propose what we have labelled as the individualised/personal and the communal/wider paradigms for analysing value positions. Within the framework of the individualised/personal paradigm, we offer a framework that limits the evaluation of value positions to their impact on and relevance to individuals. In this context, a personal value paradigm will seek to explore judgements about what ought to be included in the curriculum for an individual and what individuals ought to be learning. In contrast, the communal paradigm is extended to look at the same questions but in the context of the wider society. What should we be including in the curriculum for different groups within the society? Who ought to decide those things that are valuable for us to learn as a society?

There is no doubt that the two paradigms are most likely to yield different outcomes. Let us assume that an individual within the society has the chance to study a curriculum on walking on one's head. If judgements about the value of such a curriculum were to be made by the individual, there is no doubt that he or she will be able to provide arguments as to why learning to walk on one's head is a useful and worthwhile activity. By contrast, if a policymaker, who is making this judgement on behalf of not only the self, but also the society with the inevitable impact of cost, it is most probable that the judgement would be negative and would consider this endeavour as worthless.

As illustrated through this example, therefore, the conflict that often emanates in any discussion on value positions in education is largely informed by the framework employed in the analysis. The key question should be: is this being subjected to an individualised framework or a communal framework of analysis? What ideological leaning underpins the analysis? The truth is that answers to these questions are likely to offer us a near-accurate prediction of what our judgement is likely to be.

DOI: 10.1057/9781137535115.0002

Educational value positions in the personalised paradigm

Although we have tried to separate two different frameworks to which we could subject the analysis of value frameworks, we do not suggest that the different applications of the two frameworks in different contexts are mutually exclusive. Indeed, we suggest that it is often a question of convenience and relevance. If one were to be interested in looking at the value position held by individuals, it would seem that it is natural to select the individualised framework. Similarly, if one were to be interested in evaluating the aggregate value position held within a society, it again seems natural to employ the communal framework. However, it is not impossible to use either framework interchangeably and indeed, it would seem that this has happened repeatedly in the literature. Nonetheless, we shall now try and set out the value positions associated with the individualised framework.

A good starting point in this context is to explain the rationale behind the individualised framework. We emphasise that our suggestions here relate centrally to the provision of justification of value positions in the context of what should constitute the content of education. As we have suggested earlier, the foci of philosophy of education goes beyond a singular domain and as such we do not suggest that the analysis here could necessarily be replicated for other domains.

The individualised paradigm

At the heart of the individualised framework are two clear notions of man as a living and thinking being:

1 'Man' (human beings) has intuition about right and wrong, good and bad.
2 'Man' (human beings) has a particular nature which informs all his (our) decisions.

It is around these two features of 'man' (human beings) that the individualised framework of value position is built. Developing from the first feature is the value position that has been referred to as the intuitionist value position (see, e.g., Degenhardt, 1982; Barrow, 2013; Marples, 2011).

DOI: 10.1057/9781137535115.0002

At the heart of this value position is the assumption that the value of any educational activity is simply there. The classical argument of the key proponents of this view such as Moore (1960) and Paterson (1979) is located around two salient questions:

> First, what value should we attach to knowledge as such? 'Does knowledge figure and how does it figure?' Second, how can we establish the comparative value of different types and items of knowledge? (pp.91–92)

The answer for the holders of this value position is that we must rely on our intuition as human beings in order to provide answers to these questions. Our intuition, they argue, must be able to tell us what we ought to do and the worth of what we have decided to do.

As we suggested, the second argument around which the individualised framework is constructed is the notion that 'Man' (human beings) has a particular nature which informs all his (our) decisions. In essence, the decisions we take are informed by our very nature as human beings. For the proponents of this view, key attributes that we hold on the basis of our nature include the ability to rationalise or provide reasons (rationalism): the ability to enjoy or gain satisfaction from certain things (hedonism), the ability to be imaginative and, therefore, transpose the unknown to the known, the ability to seek, find and offer solutions to problems and the ability to facilitate self-survival. These five attributes form the core of the value positions often referred to as naturalist theories of justification. The core of this position is that our nature demands that we do things at particular times in particular ways and that the value of the decisions that we make can, therefore, be located in our natural attribute that is relevant at the particular point in time.

Describing each of the five positions presented is a well-trodden path (see, e.g., Degenhardt, 1982; Barrow, 2013; Marples, 2011) and as such we shall not be dwelling on them here. Nonetheless, we shall provide a simple definition of each value position. Rationalism is associated with the Aristotelian discussion which argues that rationality or reason is the highest value of human beings and that only our rationality holds us in contradistinction to other beings. Hedonism relates to the 18th-century concept of English utilitarianism which suggests that the value of knowledge should be judged by the degree of happiness it provides. The notion of value built around solution sees human beings as problem solvers. This is a position that has often been associated with Dewey and his argument that growth and experience should form the basis for curriculum choice,

DOI: 10.1057/9781137535115.0002

and Darwin's position that man's evolution is induced and conditioned by the need to subdue the environmental problems that surround man. The imagination argument is built around the importance of imagination to our nature and as such suggests that we ought to value and respect our imagination more highly than anything else. Finally, survivalism is built around the argument that human beings strive to subdue difficulties. As such, the value of our decision is embedded in our survival.

Of course, there are several arguments against and for all of these value positions, but that really is not our concern here. What we have tried to present is the simple argument that the value position we take can be seen to be informed by a number of arguments related directly to us as individual human beings. There are three remarks we would like to make here.

First, the essence of these value positions can be equated to what is often termed the instrumental as against the intrinsic value positions in philosophy of education. Let us consider the implications of the intuitive value of education, for instance. There is no doubt that what this value position argues for is that we should see education as having an end in itself. Education has an intrinsic value in itself and, therefore, we need not concern ourselves with the questions of 'why and what' because whatever items we have in our curriculum has a benefit that is naturally associated to it intrinsically. In contrast, the naturalist arguments tend to suggest that there is always a goal, for the achievement of which education is responsible. Education, therefore, is valuable only in as much as it is designed to achieve a goal. It is, therefore, an instrument for achieving other goals. It is within the context of its ability to achieve these goals that education can be seen to be valuable.

In the context of adult literacy, then, the crucial question is: should adult literacy be designed to enable us achieve other goals or should it be designed and seen as something simply worthwhile for its own sake? Policies and policymakers have in their own ways given an indication of their preferences in this respect. In the next chapter, what we shall be concerned with is how adult literacy policy in the United Kingdom has reflected these preferences and in some cases, how it has shifted from one value position to another.

Second, it is important to remember that it is possible for individuals to arrogate to themselves the right and the ability to make and justify these decisions on behalf of the society. In such a situation, the value of education in a society could be identified by individuals or a small group

DOI: 10.1057/9781137535115.0002

of people who would often argue that they are better able to recognise what should be valuable for the entire society.

Third, we can clearly see how the framework we have explored can be readily used in analysing value positions relevant to individuals. For example, it is easier for us to talk about the intuition of an individual rather than the intuition of an entire society. It is for this reason that we have advocated the perception of this framework as individualised.

The communal paradigm: the Human and Social Capital value positions

Educational value position in the communal sense is explored using a variety of frameworks. However, there is nothing definitive about what framework we ought to be using, as different writers have drawn on a variety of political and economic drivers to offer their preferred paradigms. Our concern is not to take a position on which of these is most adequate. Rather, our aim is to demonstrate that value positions can be framed within the context of an overall framework of benefits to the society at large rather than to individuals. In this context, therefore, we have opted to take a brief look at what might be called the capitals paradigm. In recent years, the value of education policies at the societal or communal level is often framed in the context of the Human Capital value position as against the Social Capital value position. Certainly, these two have become one of the most influential positions which inform the analysis of educational policies (Fitzsimons, 1999; Dae-Bong, 2009). Human Capital may be viewed from a micro-perspective, for example, the way the accumulation of knowledge and skills, such as literacy practices, enables learners to increase their productivity and their earnings. At the macro level, the focus is usually on how this impacts on the productivity and wealth of the communities and societies they live. The dominant model of institutional literacies derives Human Capital from economic returns, such as employability. Therefore, the impetus created by the Human Capital position seeks to connect educational systems to neo-liberal economic development strategies such that knowledge and learning are now positioned as modes of capital with the main goal being the contribution of education to productivity. Hence, the value of education is inherent in its contributions to productivity. As a result, decisions about what we ought to be teaching and learning, what ought to be in

DOI: 10.1057/9781137535115.0002

our curricula, must be framed in the context of the overall economic benefit to the entire society.

In contrast, an alternative argument, the Social Capital, is presented in contradistinction to the Human Capital argument (see, e.g., Coleman, 1988; Bourdieu, 1986; Fukuyama, 1995). Social Capital distances itself to some extent from the economic indices valued by the Human Capital argument. According to Bourdieu (1991, p.118), Social Capital prefers to acknowledge resources that are available to individuals because individuals possess 'a durable network of more or less institutionalised relationships of mutual acquaintance and recognition'. This ties in with Coleman's (1988, p.595) description of an intellectual stream, whose virtues lie in 'its ability to describe action in social context and to explain the way action is shaped, constrained and redirected by social context'. These two positions, then, constitute the core of the debate on what the value of education should be. In a way, they represent the argument of the instrumental as against the intrinsic value of education. For the former, the value of education is embodied in what it is able to contribute to the economy of both the society and the individual. It should thus be seen as an instrument of promoting economic development. In contrast, the latter limits the benefit more to the individual and indeed, to the natural end that education could generate of its own accord.

Conclusion

Given the goals set out within the framework of these value positions, we can see with clarity how the analysis of the value of education in the communal sense is best carried out using this framework. Although it is possible to explore the value to individuals using this framework, it is obvious that it can be better utilised in the context of value to the society rather than to the individual. In the context of adult literacy education and the policies that drive its practice, therefore, it is possible to investigate their value in the context of whether we see adult literacy in the context of what it might be able to contribute to the economy at a societal level or what it might be able to contribute to the individual as an end in itself. Should adult literacy be seen as valuable if it helps to promote the job prospect of learners and, therefore, contribute to the economy, or should it be seen as a means of deriving and offering satisfaction in its own right? We offer no specific answer to these questions. What we aim

DOI: 10.1057/9781137535115.0002

to show in the next chapter is how the driving perception has continued to shift from one value position to the other and to illustrate this shift with policies that represent the shifting value positions.

Notes

1   Illustrating the multi-dimensional import of philosophy, Duckworth (2013, p.14) drew on a wider sociological engagement with issues of violence, when exploring intersectionality approaches to recognising multiple oppressions as shaping women's experiences of education and literacy highlighting how structural inequalities such as class impact on the women over the course of their life and how they find ways to survive.

2   For example, Ramesh (2015) notes in the *Guardian* that 'to justify the cuts, the Tories are likely to employ a narrative of skivers v strivers, suggesting a clear division between a large, permanently welfare-dependent group and the rest of the population who pay taxes to support it. The Tories know this is a fiction, but it is a politically useful one.'

3   For example, not least because of the growing inequality and lack of meritocracy. A recent study identified that a child of a higher professional or managerial father is 20 times more likely to end up in high status job than a child with a working-class father (Bukodi et al., 2015). These figures are indeed troubling.

DOI: 10.1057/9781137535115.0002

2
Changing Value Positions: A Movement in Transition

Abstract: *Drawing on philosophical, sociological and economic lenses, this chapter tracks the value positions that could be associated with the changing policies and events in the field of adult literacy in the United Kingdom over the past four decades. We commence the analysis of policy evolution from the 1970s, largely because this was the period when adult literacy started filtering into policy discourse. The analysis will be constructed around three broad periods: the 1970s to the early 1980s, the early 1980s to the mid-1990s and the mid-1990s through Moser to date. The blocks are not arbitrary, as they are informed by major policy events and pronouncements. In analysing each period, although there will be a recording of historical facts, the major focus will be on the perceived underpinning values informing policy direction, as well as the implication for practice which includes the vocationalisation and marketisation of the literacy provision.*

Keywords: adult literacy; marketisation; philosophy; policy; sociology of education

Ade-Ojo, Gordon and Vicky Duckworth. *Adult Literacy Policy and Practice: From Intrinsic Values to Instrumentalism.* Basingstoke: Palgrave Macmillan, 2015. DOI: 10.1057/9781137535115.0003.

Introduction

In this chapter, our goal is to track the value positions that could be associated with the changing policies and events in the field of adult literacy
in the United Kingdom over the past four decades. Before exploring this
process of evolution, we want to make the following remarks as a form
of guideline for understanding our approach here.

First, we do not suggest that there is a direct one-to-one match
between policies and value positions. As a result, in many cases, we
subject the relationship to our own analysis and interpretation. This,
might, therefore, not be a universal perception of the ways in which
events have unfolded.

Second, in some of the stages in the evolution of adult literacy in the
United Kingdom, there were no explicit policy positions which were
directly focused on adult literacy. In such cases, we have drawn on what
we consider to be relevant events and activities rather than policies.

Third, we have classified the stages in the evolution into three main
periods; the 1970s, the 1980s to mid-1990s and the mid-1990s. We also
explored in a limited sense the post-Moser years. It is legitimate to question this categorisation. Why have we classified the stages in this particular
way? Our answer is simple, because of the particular nature of policy
direction in each of these periods. Policy events and activities in the first
period shared one commonality: the significant influence of the voluntary
sector, which meant that policy was substantially led by practice. The
second period was carved out because policy activities, events and statements during this period were not directly focused on adult literacy.
Rather, although they had relevance for adult literacy practice, they were
essentially located in other areas which inadvertently impacted upon adult
literacy practice. This period is, therefore, seen as an era in which adult
literacy policy developed more through coincidence than through intent.
The third period was carved out because it was a period during which adult
literacy gained full recognition as a field of education and was considered
worthy of specific policy pronouncements. It is, therefore, seen as a period
of adult literacy policy with conscious intent on the part of policymakers.

Fourth, our analysis in this chapter draws on the two frameworks of
values we discussed in the previous chapter. In particular, we see the
concepts of intrinsic and instrumental value positions as common to
both frameworks. As such, our analysis will reference both of these value
positions regardless of the framework we draw from.

DOI: 10.1057/9781137535115.0003

Finally, in order to reinforce our arguments in this chapter, we shall draw from the data collected from a previous study on adult literacy policy, which was collected through the interview of former and current practitioners and members of a policy development team in the area of adult literacy language and numeracy. Although we shall be explicitly making our own claims about events and policies, we shall draw on comments from these participants to support some of our claims when necessary.

The 1970s

Adult literacy has a long history, but has particularly grown in prominence during the past three decades. We start with a rather bold claim here; the 1970s started with an alignment to the intrinsic values of education but as the decade developed, there is evidence that the instrumental value position began to take control. Using the communal framework, we again make the bold claim that the 1970s was initially driven by the value position of social capital, but later became engulfed in a human capital ethos. To support these bold claims, we shall now look at some of the quasi-policies and events that took place during this period.

Many scholars have described the 1970s as lacking a definitive literacy policy particularly from the perspective of the state. Putting this lack of distinct policy in the 1970s into context, Limage (1987, p.293) notes:

> To dignify the types of national commitment to eradicating adult literacy with the term 'policy' can, at best, leave adult literacy tutors, organisers, and activists somewhat perplexed.

In contrast, others see the mid-1970s as the period during which adult literacy began to assume a national policy dimension. For instance, Hamilton (2001, p.24) notes:

> Adult literacy was first identified as a national policy issue in the UK in the mid-1970s; prior to this there had neither been the widespread perception of lack of literacy skills amongst adults, nor the level of provision necessary to rectify such a problem.

Whichever side of the debate one takes, it is apparent that policy initiatives in the 1970s originated from, and were driven mostly by, non-governmental stakeholders. In essence, the 1970s could be classified

DOI: 10.1057/9781137535115.0003

as an era of practice-driven policy, in which a myriad of initiatives originated from practitioners and their funders in the most part. A range of events and factors within the society, therefore, stood in place of conventional policy and provide evidence for the justification of our claims in terms of the underpinning values. What we analyse, therefore, includes a combination of events initiated by both government agencies and voluntary organisations.

Perhaps the first of a series of significant events/quasi-policies in the evolution of literacy policy and practice in the 1970s was the publication of the Russell Report on adult education. Some of the relevant recommendations of the report include the need for increased expenditure and the desirability of greater cooperation between local education authorities (LEAS) and other agencies to provide for 'disadvantaged people' (Russell, 1973; Fieldhouse, 1996; Fowler, 2005). Although the Russell Report did not focus essentially on the development of literacy, it identified a new group of citizens that demanded the attention of both the government and the citizenry in general. Central to this is the identification of what was then referred to as 'the disadvantaged adult'. Interviewees who were practitioners in the 1970s, but have remained researchers, policymakers and managers opined that the real importance of the Russell Report was its identification of the category that is generally referred to as 'the disadvantaged adult'.

Another significant event was the British Association of Settlers (henceforth BAS) series of campaign activities, which ultimately generated the interests of individuals and organisations. The BAS, it can be argued, kick-started the development of literacy policy and practice during this period. The first significant contribution of BAS was the execution of a national survey, which quantified the extent of literacy problem (Hamilton and Hillier, 2006). This served as a launching pad for its campaign on entitlement. Following on the heels of this survey was the launch of the Right to Read campaign (RRD). The RRD campaign was essentially initiated by a charter, which 'demanded that the government of the United Kingdom undertake a commitment to eradicate adult illiteracy by a reasonable date, in particular, 1985' (Limage, 1987, p.302). It is important that we put into perspective the role of BAS at this time against the backdrop of the social reality within which they operated. Limage describes the social terrain of the British society with the metaphor of 'two nations on the verge of confrontation, the labouring poor and the wealthy middle class, which voluntary bodies sought

DOI: 10.1057/9781137535115.0003

to reconcile' (p.302). The BAS was one of such voluntary bodies which were created with this goal in mind. Thus, it becomes clear that the foundational ethos of BAS was essentially those of entitlement, catering for the disadvantaged and in essence, therefore, that of social responsibility. The involvement of the BAS in the literacy campaign was not a one-off. Indeed, they brought into this campaign a range of experience from other campaigns with the similar theme of entitlement and helping the disadvantaged.

Also significant in the context of literacy policy and practice development in the 1970s were the series of broadcasting programmes developed by the British Broadcasting Corporation (henceforth BBC). Ostensibly, the role of the BBC in the evolution of literacy policy in the 1970s was essentially focused on publicity. Hamilton and Hillier (2006, p.9), in line with this perception, note that '[t]here were very important links between the British association of settlements (BAS) and the BBC who publicised the issue and pushed for the development of local responses'.

The contributions of the BBC manifested in a number of activities that are discussed in the pages that follow. In the aftermath of the announcement of 'Status Illiterate: Prospect Zero' by the BAS in 1973, the campaign document, 'A Right to Read', was released in 1974. At about the same time, the BBC announced its intention to launch a three-year project of radio and television broadcasting programmes (Moorhouse, 1983). Those reading this book, who were around at the time, may remember actor Bob Hoskins, the lorry driver who fronted the images. What these broadcasting components contributed essentially were the provision of an organ of publicity for potential literacy students and for the group that eventually became the core of practitioners: volunteer tutors. According to Moorhouse (1982), the BBC announcements 'added a valuable urgency to the growing campaign' (p.233). The timing of the BBC broadcast series was seen as very significant in at least one respect. Moorhouse (1982) notes that the BBC's broadcast at this time 'brought forward many new volunteers in time for at least a proportion of them to be trained before students came asking for help' (p.235).

Equally significant as a contribution towards the development of literacy was the BBC's role in the development of resources. In the autumn of 1975, the BBC began a radio series called 'Teaching Adults to Read'. The goal of this series was to introduce beginner volunteers to the job of adult literacy teaching. This series, it can be argued, contributed to the development of tutors in rural areas in particular. Considering the fact

DOI: 10.1057/9781137535115.0003

that many volunteers in rural areas did not have too many opportunities to meet for training, recorded versions of these broadcasts were effectively utilised in the induction of beginner teachers. Complementing the broadcast series was the BBC Adult Literacy Handbook, which was designed as an all-purpose reference book on different aspects of literacy.

Following its initial 'On the Move' series, which was launched in the autumn of 1975, a more advanced series of the same title was launched in October 1976 and repeated between 1977 and 1978. The original 'On the Move' series comprised 50 ten-minute programmes, screened thrice weekly and focused on sensitising potential learners to the fact that their problems were in fact not unique to them alone. This was in addition to the focus of providing information on the nature of literacy problems. The more advanced series that the BBC started broadcasting in 1976 lasted 25 minutes per episode and were screened at weekly intervals. Accompanying these series were a students' workbook and notes for tutors.

The radio component of the BBC's contribution, labelled 'Next Move', was launched in the spring of 1977. The series comprised ten-minute readings of tailor-made materials and was delivered with the aid of an accompanying workbook to follow while listening. More inadvertently than by design, the first phase in what some might today call blended learning originated from the BBC's involvement with the adult literacy campaign. Subsequently, the BBC extended its project to include development and publication of a range of programmes and materials. More importantly, the BBC's effort was considered effective and seen as pivotal in getting well over 100,000 adults with literacy problems to come forward.

The events reviewed were essentially driven neither by organisations that were government education agencies nor by government policies. A central focus of these events was the issue of entitlement. There were no specific expectations in terms of what type of literacy adults needed to acquire. Indeed, decisions as to what needs to be learned, when and where were mostly taken by the learners. A key question here is what sort of value position would drive literacy for disadvantaged adults and for entitlement? Although the events were effectively silent on this question, in the context of that silence, one can assume that the goal was simply to empower these adults so that they can reap the intrinsic benefits of literacy. As such, we suggest that this was an indication that the relevant

DOI: 10.1057/9781137535115.0003

value associated with literacy in the Russell Report, for example, was more intrinsic than instrumental. From the viewpoint of our communal framework, we again suggest that the driver was more about social capital than about the human capital. As the decade progressed, however, the government began to become more involved in policy development. In a way, that involvement also signals the beginning of a movement in transition, a gradual shift from one value position to another.

The emergence of governmental agencies and policies

A landmark quasi-policy development at this stage was the allocation of what was then a huge amount of money, one million pounds, to the development of adult literacy. Perhaps the most significant impact of the unprecedented allocation of fund for the development of literacy was the attendant establishment of Adult Literacy Resource Agency (ALRA), which was charged with the distribution and monitoring of the allocated funds. While it has been noted that the allocated fund was limited and that the projection for ALRA was itself short-term and interim in nature (Fowler, 2005; Hamilton and Hillier, 2006), it is significant to note that this was the first time that a quasi-governmental agency had been given a supervisory role in the context of literacy development. More importantly, the establishment of ALRA, which in turn morphed into Adult Literacy Unit (ALU), which subsequently morphed into Adult Literacy and Basic Skills Unit (ALBSU) and ultimately became the Basic Skills Agency (BSA), signified the introduction of an instrumentalist value position. In this regard, the value of any adult literacy programme now rests with the judgement of this monitoring agency, rather than the learners. Effectively, therefore, the allocation of fund initiated a process which ultimately was to become highly significant in the development of policy and practice in adult literacy. The transformation from one organisation to another was accompanied by a commensurate alteration in the remit of the organisation. Hamilton (1996, p.152) captures this series of transformations when she notes that where ALRA was concerned, 'it began as a resource agency, but became more of a monitoring and quality control body'. For us, therefore, the provision of a dedicated fund and the subsequent creation of ALRA signalled the beginning of a movement in transition. In place of an intrinsic value which had learners at its heart, a gradual journey into the realm of instrumentalism was initiated.

DOI: 10.1057/9781137535115.0003

The establishment of the Manpower Service commission (MSC) with its remit to provide for and fund youth training schemes, as well as work-related initiatives in schools, is another significant event in the evolution of adult literacy policy. Although the MSC was set up in 1973 and actually commenced full operations in January 1974, before the first formal literacy campaign, it played an important role in shaping the direction of literacy practice and policy particularly in the later part of the 1970s and the 1980s. In the context of our analysis of value positions, the significance of the existence and role of the MSC is underscored by the following factors. First, the MSC at a later stage in its existence provided the first framework for offering adult literacy as a form of remedial course for employment skills. In this context, the MSC provided funding for full-time adult literacy and numeracy courses for candidates who were deemed unequipped to pass its TOPS courses, or unable to sustain their jobs because of their limited levels of literacy and numeracy (Fowler, 2005). Thus, the notion of adult literacy as an instrument for achieving the goal of employability skills was first introduced through the MSC.

The second area in which the significance of the involvement of the MSC is manifested is in the area of funding and its attendant concepts of selection and monitoring. As noted by Hamilton (1996), involvement of MSC signalled the first time that a full basic skill course would be funded. However, in order to qualify for these courses, a certain level of skills was necessary. This demand for qualifications, perhaps more appropriately put, skills, signalled the introduction of selection in the provision of literacy. In a way, it signalled a departure from providing literacy to meet the needs of the people to a framework of providing literacy to meet the perceived needs of the government.

Closely related to the issue of selection is the introduction of a monitoring regime. By its very remit, the MSC was set up to address the employment and skills needs. When it ventured into the literacy terrain, it became inevitable that the central plank of its operations, upgrading the skills of the unskilled, is imported into the provision of literacy. As a result, the MSC lost interest in the existing welfarist agenda that was initially all-pervading in the provision of literacy. Rather, it was interested mainly in training adults for employment purposes. This compels an inevitable perception of adult literacy as a means to an end. This, then, was the beginning of a centralised form of curriculum and the

DOI: 10.1057/9781137535115.0003

introduction of a monitoring regime in the development of adult literacy policy and practice.

The foregoing is an attempt at highlighting a series of events, not exhaustive by any means, which in different ways contributed to, and shaped the direction of literacy policy and practice development in the 1970s. While an attempt has been made to identify and discuss the impact that these events had on the literacy practice and policy, our main goal is to show that these events constituted a manifestation of different value positions. The earlier years with the involvement of non-governmental agencies paint a picture of a value position that recognises the intrinsic value of education. There were no specified expected outcomes from the government.

Not surprisingly, however, with growing governmental involvement, it would seem that policy in the later part of the decade began to shift towards an instrumental value position. Government agencies such as ALRA and MSC began to insist on specific outcomes which saw literacy as a means to an end. Using the communal model of the capital framework appears to be the most fruitful way of analysing this movement in the evolutionary process of value positions in adult literacy. One of the central features of the human capital value position is the expectation that education must have some value in economic terms. That value, in this context, can manifest in the perceived worth of having an education. In the context of the setting in the 1970s, it is obvious that as the decade progressed, literacy began to be valued in terms of what it could contribute with regard to employment. Employment thus became a key driver in the shaping of the direction and dimension of adult literacy policy and practice.

In contrast, the earlier part of the decade and the activities that symbolised the direction of adult literacy did not recognise economic outcomes as central to the shape of literacy. Indeed, the notions of entitlement and the disadvantaged adult primarily echoed the social capital ethos of building support networks amongst others. As such, the expectation was not on the financial outcomes that adult literacy could yield, but on the value that it possesses in terms of helping the recipients to build their own network of support.

A relevant question in this context might then be why governmental involvement tended to end the influence of the social capital value position. Of significance in the context of social responsibility and entitlement was the reality of radicalism that was beginning to be pronounced within

DOI: 10.1057/9781137535115.0003

the society. There was a groundswell of radical behaviours, which was beginning to be a source of concern to society at large. McKenzie (2001, p.215), in analysing this period, notes that there was '[e]scalating public fears about the behaviours of certain groups of people, including teachers, young people and black youth in particular'. While this observation appears to focus on youths, there is no doubt that it was an issue that pervaded the entire society, and not in any particular age-driven pattern.

The response to this state of event can be viewed from two dimensions and correlates to two different but related strains of socio-cognitive themes, which influenced the evolution of adult literacy policy and practice. While on the one hand the government probably sees this as some form of irresponsibility, others within the society saw it from the viewpoint of the disadvantaged group and a question of entitlement. For those who hold the latter position, the lack of literacy skills is one of the reasons for the seemingly errant patterns of behaviour that has been noticed in the society. Many people, at least one million, in the conservative estimate of the BAS, were seen to have literacy needs. In the views of those who hold this position, therefore, the rights of these disadvantaged people to education, their entitlements within the structure of the society, had hitherto been denied them. This, in a way, sets the scene for a conflict, which not only manifested in the opinions of relevant people, but also in the influential value position that drove policy. Inevitably, the value position held by the government came out on top.

Comments from practitioners in the 1970s who have remained in the field in different roles confirm our perception of the dominant value positions. Talking about the BAS, one interviewee describes them as:

> well they were a kind of missionary group, weren't they, I mean...this idea that the universities should have some kind of connection with their communities, and they should be going out and doing good things, and sharing culture and sharing knowledge, those are very missionary kind of approach to things.

This notion of 'doing good' encapsulates in a way the essence of the theme of catering for the disadvantaged, who were then seen as needing the 'good things' that should naturally be available to them. Elaborating further on the notion of entitlement, the same respondent says: 'I think there was a kind of established view at the time that people who'd missed out on education the first time should have an entitlement to, you know, a second chance as it was known.'

DOI: 10.1057/9781137535115.0003

Another interviewee spoke of the perception of people's entitlement in order to support them in achieving their goals. According to this respondent, many people became involved on the back of the BAS campaign, and,

> I suppose quite militant in a fairly, sort of small 'm' militant, with a small 'm' about making more and more opportunities available for people to pursue what they wanted to pursue, without having to pay for it, because it was an entitlement.

Another practitioner interviewed noted:

> Literacy is a basic right to which everyone is entitled. This may be a somewhat well-worn phrase but in fact the concept behind it is fundamental to the purpose and approach of the British association of Settlements Literacy campaign. We do regard literacy as a right and in the final analysis we feel it is the responsibility of local education to provide facilities which will ensure that literacy skills may be acquired. (BAS, 1973, p.1)

The perception expressed in the responses mentioned is not far from the position held by BAS (1974), which saw it from the viewpoint of 'civic right necessary for a fulfilled life within society'. In their official bulletin, BAS declared:

> We believe that the power for social action depends on the ability to handle communications. In order to participate, to exercise certain rights, to choose between alternatives and to solve problems, people need certain basic skills: listening, talking, reading and writing. (p.2)

Similar sentiments have been expressed by researchers and record keepers. For instance, Catherine Moorhouse (1983) who was the director of the Inner London Education Authority Language and Literacy Unit between 1974 and 1979 describes the literacy campaign of the 1970s as being confining itself 'to claims in terms of functional literacy as a basic human right' (p.145).

Opinions, such as the one provided by Moorhouse quoted earlier, confirm the viewpoint that the notion of entitlement, viewed from a perception of individual rights, was indeed a powerful factor in the evolution of literacy policy and practice in the 1970s.

With a slight shade to it, another interviewee introduced the notion of 'public duty', commenting that:

> I think it was the BBC interpreting its public duty charter and wanting to take that forward. And I think this literacy stuff was the beginning of, um, phone in to advice things, ... I think it was an initiative from them.

DOI: 10.1057/9781137535115.0003

Another variant of the concept of entitlement manifested itself in the consciousness of some of the activists in the notion of representation. As one interviewee notes:

> but there's also another term I found actually is quite helpful, as a critical term to review it with, is to say it was on behalf 'ist work. There was a lot of, to start with, campaigning on behalf of a population.

Others project the notions of 'what should be rightfully available to the general public'. Illustrating this is this comment:

> That most activists and practitioners were driven into this by their perception of what should rightfully be available to the general public and their own sense of social responsibility is beyond a doubt. Yes there were other factors, but these two must take a pride of place. The BBC's involvement epitomises this. It was as if they decided through one or two people that the organisation had the duty to help people get what they were entitled to and that it was their own (at least those involved) responsibility to ensure that this happened.

The vital link between these comments in terms of the initial government participation and the notion of social responsibility is in this case an indirect one. Deriving from the argument that one of the reasons for the BBC's involvement was social responsibility, and the fact that it was through the BBC's involvement that an effective threat was generated to 'shame' or coerce the government into participating, we can argue that in an indirect way, the government's participation was informed by the notion of social responsibility. The crucial issue, however, is the level of awareness and degree of consciousness of government representatives. How really aware were they of the agenda that was being driven by the BBC and BAS? On the basis of the analysis carried out, we suggest that the non-governmental agencies such as the BBC and BAS were driven by a social capital value position which manifested mostly in the context of entitlement and social responsibility. By happenstance, however, and to a very limited extent, government agencies appeared to have at least aided them if furthering the course of their work in the area of adult literacy. It is important to note that this was possible at the time because there were no designated government agencies with responsibility for this area of work. As we suggested earlier, work in this area was dictated by practice which was in effect largely directed by voluntary organisations. In effect, the predominance of a social capital value position was enhanced because of the synergy between the value of voluntary organisations and the tenets of the social capital value position.

DOI: 10.1057/9781137535115.0003

Rationales for the value positions in the evolution of literacy policy and practice the 1970s

As was the case with various spheres of education in the 1970s, the factors of employment and the economy played a significant role in the direction of policy on literacy. The social reality at this point in time reflects a growing concern about the rate of unemployment with unemployment inevitably linked to its economic repercussions. Many commentators have noted that unemployment was not simply a phenomenon that emerged of its own accord (Habermas, 1975; McKenzie, 2001). Rather, unemployment was itself a direct result of the global economic problem that confronted many industrialised nations in the mid-1970s. Emphasising the importance of the economic factor in the 1970s, McKenzie (2001, p.215) notes that:

> the worsening national and global economic crisis had a profound effect on attitudes during the 1970s. In 1973 and 1974 there were dramatic international rises in oil prices, which have often been associated with the start of a recession in the UK.

And by the mid-1970s,

> economic issues had become most uppermost in political debates, as economic crisis followed economic crisis, and by the end of the 1970s, the crisis was dominating all aspects of government.

The overall outcome of this series of economic crisis as she again notes in conjunction with Habermas (1975) was that '[u]nemployment increased to over one million and governments seemed to be facing a legitimation crisis'. From the foregoing, it became very difficult to discuss unemployment as a factor without anchoring it to its root, the economic crisis. This is particularly important because it brings into focus the differing visions, and the different ways in which different parties responded to the crisis of unemployment, and how their responses have contributed in different ways to the value positions that drove the evolution of literacy policy and practice.

The government's response to the general problem of economic recession and the attendant unemployment in particular was significantly different from those of other organs within the society. This difference is particularly manifested in the value positions associated with adult literacy policy and practice development. Where the government was

DOI: 10.1057/9781137535115.0003

concerned, the fundamental impact of this social reality was the notion of the welfare state being overburdened. As noted by Halsey et al. (1980; Cited in McKenzie, 2001, p.6) and Hargreaves (1994, p.3), respectively, education was treated as 'the wastebasket of society' and 'policy receptacles into which society's unsolved and unsolvable problems are unceremoniously deposited'.

Allen and Ainley (2007) perceive the response of the government from a different angle. In their view, the response of the government in the United Kingdom was to adopt the globally trendy 'human capital theory' approach to education' (p.15). They note that:

> Although education and training continued to be organised in different ways in different countries, there was general agreement across Western governments that education should be seen as a form of investment. (p.15)

The ultimate goal, therefore, was to design a new construct of education as a panacea for the economic ailments of the society. This pattern of reasoning was in a way embraced by the fledgling adult literacy field. This signalled the introduction of economic considerations into the field and initiated the regime of what later became known as a value-for-money approach to education. Thus, the government confronted the issue of unemployment from the viewpoint of educational inadequacies and effectively transferred this into the process of policy development. McKenzie (2001) sheds further light on this position, observing that:

> Education provided a neat and simplistic focus for otherwise disparate and complex discontents. Social trends such as mass unemployment, aging populations and changes to the traditional family meant that governments were also becoming overburdened by their responsibilities for social welfare. This provided a supportive environment for the monetarist policies of the New Right (involving cuts in educational spending) and its associated moral underclass discourse (failure in education being discussed in terms of personal inadequacies rather than un-equal life chances. (p.6)

In effect, the response of the government was to associate a huge chunk of societal problems, including unemployment, with the inadequacies of members of the society. In particular, members of the underclass, which included to a large extent those who were described as 'illiterate' were considered responsible for the economic problems of the society. It follows logically, therefore, that the government's position was to view the issue of unemployment from the perspective of skills development. Failure in education was seen in some way as failing the nation (Ball, 1990).

DOI: 10.1057/9781137535115.0003

Encapsulating this perception is the speech given by the then Labour Party leader, James Callaghan, at Ruskin College, Oxford, in which he declared:

> I am concerned on my journeys to find complaints from industry that new recruits from schools sometimes do not have the basic tools to do the job that is required. (McKenzie, 2001, p.215)

He goes further to emphasise the value of skills, presumably as against knowledge, by declaring that 'there is no virtue in producing socially well-adjusted members of the society who are unemployed because they do not have the skills' (p.125). The focus, therefore, was on how to meet the needs and the demands of the industry and not those of the members of the society. The pivotal issue was what people can do to enable them meet the needs of the industry rather than what can be done to enable people meet their own needs.

The twin positions of the inadequately skilled and the need for education to serve the needs of the economy were thus the central plank upon which the government's response to the social realities of economic recession and the attendant unemployment in terms of its overall adult education policy development was built. While the government's response was to see the 'unskilled and illiterate' as constituting a significant part of the cause of the economic and unemployment crisis, others, particularly voluntary organisations and practitioners, prefer to see it as an indication of the failure of society to adequately prepare 'the disadvantaged' to cope with the dire situation. They, therefore, preferred an approach to this crisis that holds the viewpoint of empowering 'the disadvantaged'.

Although it is plain that there was a difference between the government and others in terms of their appreciation of the economic and unemployment factors, there is some evidence that both sides of the divide embraced the notion of literacy as a tool for upgrading skills in order to improve the state of employability. On the part of the government, two organisations played a very significant role in the imputation of the economic and unemployment factors into the development of policy and practice in the field of adult literacy. In the case of the non-governmental actors, however, the introduction of the themes of unemployment and economic stringency was paradoxically embodied in voluntary organisations like BAS, and many practitioners who in some cases were unwillingly seduced into this viewpoint by the constraints of funding.

DOI: 10.1057/9781137535115.0003

When the BAS started its campaign in the mid-1970s, the focus was essentially on the needs of the disadvantaged as identified by individuals within the group. By 1978, however, there is evidence that the position of BAS had shifted to include the perception of literacy as a means towards an end of skill for employment. In a letter written to the then secretary of state for education, Margaret Thatcher, the BAS through its development officer Geoffrey Clarkson declared that their conference of March 1978 was for 'a target audience from the industry and commerce having regard to the special relationship between illiteracy and unskilled jobs' (Archive document 6, p.2). This contrasts with the earlier perceptions of the goals of the literacy campaign as declared in their charter, which states that:

> Literacy is a right to which everyone is entitled...the concept behind it is fundamental to the purpose and approach of the British Association of Settlements Literacy Campaign. (BAS, 1974, p.2)

But by far more significant is the role of governmental agencies in factoring the themes of employment and economic well-being of the society into the equation of adult literacy policy and practice development. Evidence from interviewees and some existing primary data sources appear to confirm this. As recorded by a number of authors, as time went on, the MSC became increasingly influential in educational policy development and implementation (see Field, 1996; Hamilton and Hillier, 2006; Allen and Ainley, 2007). The ascendancy of the MSC reflected significantly on the evolution of policy and practice in literacy. In particular, the introduction of Pre-TOPS literacy courses initiated the process of tying literacy directly to employment skills and the process of measuring input against output in educational literacy provision.

One of the most influential actors in this respect was ALRA and its inheritors. Opinions and positions expressed in several of its publications confirm the view that the agency wholeheartedly embraced the significance of the economic/employment factors. This is particularly significant because ALRA was the official monitoring organ of adult literacy policy and practice. It was inevitable, then, that factors which conditioned the socio-cognitive realities of the organisation will have a huge impact in shaping literacy policy and practice.

In an opinion expressed in one of its newsletters, it declared that:

> Literacy is the way in to a world of new opportunities both in employment and in family life. In a literate society, being illiterate is a massive handicap. The education service must do all it can to remove it. (ALRA, 1976, 8, p.4)

DOI: 10.1057/9781137535115.0003

It is evident through this that as early as 1976, the notion of literacy for employment was already creeping into the consciousness of ALRA, and that it was inevitable that this would inform their contribution to the development of policy and practice. In the same publication cited, this notion of literacy for employment was further reiterated by ALRA when it declares that:

> Literacy is an essential tool of vocational education and training and allocations of money could, we believe, validly be used to extend the provision for adult literacy in the vocational context. (p.4).

This position was echoed in other publications by ALRA and its subsequent inheritors, ALU and ALBSU. In its January 1977 issue, ALRA declares: 'The importance and value in forging strong, though sensitive links between the adult literacy service and the industry cannot be overemphasised' (1977, 9, p.4). This theme was carried over to the days of ALBSU, which was morphed from the existing ALRA. In a number of reflective declarations at the beginning of the 1980s, ALBSU newsletters provide evidence of the existing and continuing commitment to the theme of employability through literacy. For example, in its September/ October 1980 issue, ALBSU admits that the unit's remit of:

> provision designed to improve the standard of proficiency for adults whose first or second language is English, in the areas of literacy and numeracy and those related [to] communication skills without which people are impeded from applying or being considered for employment may seem confusing for those used to seemingly simple adult literacy remits. (ALBSU, 1980, 3, p.1)

In the same publication, ALBSU highlights a range of collaborative activities with the MSC on its TOPS and YOPS courses, all focusing on the theme of employability and improving the economy. It concludes by declaring that:

> undoubtedly, a substantial programme of educational and training opportunities is urgently needed on a scale commensurate with the present level of unemployment. If only 6% of the unemployed lacked basic education, it would represent 120,000 people. (p.1)

From this it becomes obvious that by the later part of the 1970s, the instrumentalist/human capital value positions driven by the themes of unemployment and its progenitor, economic stringency, were beginning to assume very significant roles in the shaping of adult literacy policy and practice. More than any others, these themes were introduced through

DOI: 10.1057/9781137535115.0003

the socio-cognitive realities of organisations and practitioners, but were driven predominantly by organisations such as MSC and ALRA and its inheritors. One interviewee puts this in perspective when she sums up the transition from the 1970s to the 1980s as follows: 'What is important about the introduction of the themes of the economy and unemployment in the context of adult literacy policy and practice is the introduction of the concepts of skills and its attendant feature of standards.'

Although we have visited the factors of unemployment, skill and the economy, it will be remiss to not look at the significance of the introduction of standards. Tracing the emergence of standards in the curriculum delivered in schools to the 1970s, Torrance (2003, p.19) cites the DES response to Callaghan's speech as signalling the introduction of curriculum standards. In response to Callaghan's speech, a government consultative document argued that:

> the time has come to try to establish generally accepted principles for the composition of the...Curriculum for all pupils...there is a need to investigate the part which might be played by a 'protected' or 'core' element of the curriculum common to all schools. (DES, 1977, p.11)

In the case of adult literacy, the identification and 'protection' of 'core' elements fell squarely in the laps of ALRA, its inheritors and the MSC, which were able to use the financial resources they control as tools of enforcement. The focus on skills brought on by the themes of unemployment and the economy impacted mostly on the curriculum. In this respect, demands were made that curricula in schools and colleges should be designed in a way that allows them to train a sizable percentage of the now unemployed workforce. As noted by Allen and Ainley (2007, p.19), employers 'demanded government replace the emphasis given by educationalists to a free thinking "liberalist curriculum" with one which for many students was to become directly related to the world of work'. These demands were acceded to by totally compliant governmental agencies like ALRA.

Allen and Ainley (2007, p.9) go further to identify the roles of centrally funded government agencies such as the MSC, who 'bypassed democratically elected local authorities to enrol school leavers on Youth Training schemes while funding work-related initiatives'. The impact of this pattern of response on the field of adult literacy was the introduction of work-related competencies in literacy, which was manifested mostly in skills-based testing. Literacy learners began to be gradually conscripted

DOI: 10.1057/9781137535115.0003

into a learning culture, which no longer addressed their needs but the perceived economic needs of the society. In a way, this served as the foundation for what was to later become a process of substituting education for economic policy (Allen and Ainley, 2007).

With the influence of the economic and employment themes, therefore, literacy policy and practice began to be dictated by an instrumentalist value position, which inevitably necessitated the notions of curriculum standards, and a process of instrumental skills rather than intrinsic knowledge development.

From the 1980s to 1997

The development of adult literacy and practice between the 1980s and 1997 is seen in different light by different people. Capturing this divergence in perception, Fowler (2005) records these. One practitioner reminisced: 'things got really good by the early 1980s', while a civil servant, declared:

> I think the movement lost steam ... about 1978 when the government lost interest ... there was no accountability and no one had any idea whether anybody learnt anything or not. And I think probably most people didn't. (p.12)

This divergence may be as a result of a lack of formalised direction of both policy and practice. Nevertheless, there were undoubtedly a number of significant events that had bearings on the evolution of literacy policy and practice. Although it is true that these events were not specifically centred on literacy, most of them had far reaching implications for the evolution of literacy policy and practice. Our central focus, however, remains on those events that are either directly linked to, or have direct repercussion for, adult literacy practice and policy development. As a result, we may have left out many events that are listed in other works, as they are not considered as having direct and significant impact on the development of policy and practice in adult literacy. In any case, what we aim to do here is to use events and policies to illustrate how there has been a shift towards instrumentalism and attempt to identify the rationales that drove this shift in value positions. What follows, therefore, is a selective discussion of significant events and policies between the 1980s and mid-1990s in the field of adult literacy policy and practice.

DOI: 10.1057/9781137535115.0003

The metamorphosis of ALRA into ALBSU

What used to be known as the Adult Literacy Resource Agency (ALRA) in the 1970s morphed into the ALBSU in 1980. The metamorphosis into ALBSU is not in itself a significant event. What is significant is the changed nature of the mandate given to ALBSU, which marked an evolution in its role in the field of adult literacy. When it was established in the 1970s, ALRA was effectively a resource agency and played this role significantly through the procreation of resources and funding of a range of adult literacy provisions under the auspices of LEAS. With its metamorphosis into ALBSU, however, the organisation assumed the role of an official voice, holding brief in proxy for the government (Fieldhouse, 1996; Fowler, 2005; Hamilton and Hillier, 2006; Hickey, 2008).

Garnett (1989) highlights the importance of the changing role of ALBSU from being an advocate for the needy into an organ of advocacy for the government. He describes it as 'the next incarnation' of ALRA, and which 'linked funding more tightly to the new government's narrowly functional ideas of the value of education' (p.2). He sums up the changing role of organisations like ALBSU with a metaphor of domestication, noting that by the turn of the decade into the 1980s, 'What has clearly happened has been that government has contained the literacy campaign, domesticated it, and fitted it in a stable check to a substantially unchanged system' (p.9). What ALBSU appeared to have been forced to do was to become a minder of the domesticated campaign.

The evolution in the role of ALBSU reflects, in a very significant way, the change in the value position that drove policy and practice development in the field of adult literacy. First, as an official voice, ALBSU in a way introduced the notion of standardisation through its regional training programmes. In effect, this marked the beginning of the end of the flexibility and freedom to improvise, which was one of the hallmarks of the adult literacy practice in the 1970s. A notion of how things should, or indeed, must be done began to creep into the equation, which had implications, not only for practice, but also for policy. With a pre-determined end, the intrinsic value position lost its influence. The value of studying adult literacy became tied into an end that has been decided by policy-makers. That end, as subsequent events show, was essentially economic. That again raises the spectre of the human capital value position and the

DOI: 10.1057/9781137535115.0003

elimination of the social capital value position. One fallout of this process of standardisation was that those who really needed help appeared to have been marginalised because the nature of the help they required did not fit the structure of the type of help the supervisory organs were willing to fund.

Closely related to this is the gradual marginalisation of the voluntary sector organs, which played such a significant role in the development of literacy policy and practice in the 1970s. The crucial point here is that these voluntary organisations played a significant role in the development of the social capital which was readily available in the early 1970s. With ALBSU taking over control through the mandate of the government, the contributions and importance of these organisations began to wane as did the social capital value position that had been so influential previously.

The importance of the changed role of ALBSU in the context of the changing value positions was the fact that it heralded the era of structured funding with its attendant target setting. Practitioners and providers in the field of adult literacy were forced to adapt to the changing institutional and funding context within which they were compelled to operate. Setting targets introduced the notion of a desired end, an end that practitioners and learners were compelled to follow. Using our individualised framework, this introduced the value position of instrumentalism. It signalled another movement in transition, again towards an instrumental destination.

The new role of ALBSU as the official voice of the government is also significant because it aided the government in driving through its agenda via its chosen agent. The incumbent conservative government was interested in basic skills (and, therefore, literacy) only in the context of the possibility that it might contribute to the process of finding solutions to the problem of a seemingly ever-increasing number of unemployed adults (Hamilton and Hillier, 2006). While this was a relatively widespread phenomenon across Europe, the assumption in England was that education in general, and literacy in particular, could be used as a remedy for this social ailment. Again, we see the influence of the instrumental as well as the human capital value positions. With the former, the value of literacy is in the fact that it can serve as a means to an end which is to help people become employable. With the latter, the value of literacy is located in what it can contribute to the economy through employment. Thus, the notion of literacy as a panacea for poor vocational development

DOI: 10.1057/9781137535115.0003

and employability began to assume prominence. Fieldhouse (1996) acknowledges this change in value position noting that:

> a very different policy rationale was in ascendance: that of economic efficiency, rather than the right to read ... public discussions about literacy increasingly invoked the vocational discourse of human resource investment.

This change in value position, in a sense, appears to draw from the overall government perspective on education, which was beginning to perceive literacy as a remedy to social problems, rather than perceive poor literacy as a symptom of a deeper underlying social malaise. At the heart of this shift in value position were employers of labour. Martin and Ainley (2007) capture the role of the industry when they observe that:

> As traditional industrial apprenticeship collapsed along with heavy industry, employers increasingly expected state schools and colleges to take responsibility for training their workforce. They demanded government replace the emphasis given by educationalists to a free thinking 'liberal humanist' curriculum with one which for many students was to be directly related to the world of work.

This pattern of using education as a tool of social engineering and correction was adopted and utilised in the field of adult literacy. Helping to implement this is ALBSU among others, although there is no evidence that this was its preferred way of doing it.

A number of comments drawn from participants in a previous related study corroborate the claims we make. One respondent concludes as follows:

> In the 1970s, the language was still about disadvantage and not yet about skills and levels quite so explicitly as it became in the 1980s I think. One strand of the 1980s was without a doubt focused on employability and unemployment.

Another noted in respect of the fund administered by ALBSU and other agencies like the MSC:

> Yeah, to access this fund, you know, the policy was kind of consciously shaped in that way, kind of say, well this is going to cater for employment, rather than just see this as people's entitlement.

Education Reform Act and the TEC White Paper 1988

Education Reform Act 1988

The Education Reform Act (ERA) is frequently described as 'the single most important piece of education legislation' (Hamilton and Hillier

DOI: 10.1057/9781137535115.0003

2006; Winch, 2000). For many who see ERA as highly significant in the development of educational policy, the importance attached to the legislation is not informed by the legislation itself, but by its consequences. In other words, it is really the aftermath of the policy that makes it so significant for many facets of education in the United Kingdom. Acknowledging the significance of the impact of this piece of legislation, Winch (2000, p.1) notes that apart from being 'the single most important piece of education legislation since the 1944 education act', it is a certainty that the legislation 'will shape the nature of our education system for the rest of this century and beyond'. The importance of the ERA was similarly acknowledged by Powell and Edwards (2005) who conclude that the 'recent increased interest in British educational provision arising from the consequences of the Education Reform Act' is essentially because 'The ERA was pivotal insofar as it precipitated what has been a relentless neo-liberal political campaign' (p.96). In our view, the key words here are 'relentless and precipitated'. The ERA is generally seen as significant because it developed a template which informed and has continued to inform the shape of educational policy and practice in different spheres within the United Kingdom.

In the case of adult literacy, this certainly was the case. Although the ERA did not have a specific focus on adult literacy, it provided a template for remodelling the policy, practice and delivery of adult literacy. According to Payne (1990, p.31), the ERA was 'a culmination of a move initiated by the department towards central direction and statutory control, particularly in curricular and assessment matters'. He goes further to describe the impetus behind the reform as:

> a strain of conservative thinking which sought to reduce the dominant role of local education and to increaser the influence of the consumers – by introducing market principles into schools.

Winch (2000) reflects a similar sentiment in terms of the appreciation of the driving political force behind the reform. Although acknowledging that other issues such as the emergence of different types of schools, the empowerment of parents and the desire to make the UK education system comparable to those of her industrial partners, the most important outcome of the reform was 'the diminution in the power of local authorities and educational experts and an increase in the power both of the state and of parents' (p.1).

DOI: 10.1057/9781137535115.0003

What comes out of the arguments cited is a picture of the emergence of regulation and standardisation as a by-product of the ERA. Indeed, the landscape of political intentions, which underpinned the ERA, presents a pattern that suggests that the desire for centralised control of education through the instruments of standardisation, testing and supervision was highly significant.

How then did this impact on the evolution of adult literacy practice and policy? In our view, what the ERA achieved was to put to the fore a New Right ideology which eliminated the notion of welfarism in education. It appears to be the recognition of the value position of anti-welfarism, which is reinforced through ERA's introduction of entrepreneurship and marketisation in education. Tomlinson (2001, p.46) notes that what was vividly outstanding about the ERA was that:

> It made the decisive break with welfare state principles (and) in contrast was about individual entrepreneurism and competitiveness, achieved through bringing education into the market place by consumer choice... It was also paradoxical about increasing the influence of the central state on education by reducing local powers and taking control of what was taught in schools.

Where adult literacy policy and practice was concerned, what the ERA did was to offer a template for the delivery and funding of literacy. Although a holistic policy in adult literacy which reflects this was to come only a few years later, the dominant discourse in the field began to mirror the dictates of the ERA, until eventually similar conditions were imposed on the field through the Further and Higher Education Act of 1992.

The emergence of the new ethos of standardisation and control helped the government to relentlessly pursue the agenda of vocationalisation in the field of adult literacy, as indeed, it has done in many other educational spheres. Government agencies such as MSC and ALBSU were instrumental in driving through this agenda. Funding for the delivery of literacy became attached to meeting set standards of delivery, evidenced by recognised accreditation, and offered only on a basis of value for money. In the field of adult literacy, therefore, the template created by the ERA heralded a clear departure from the intrinsic and social capital value position in education and their replacement with the human capital and instrumental economic-related themes of standardisation, profitability, employment and competitiveness. The advent of the ERA thus signalled the perception of education as a solution to social ills.

DOI: 10.1057/9781137535115.0003

The establishment of the TECs

Although the white paper that proposed their creation was first presented in 1988, Training and Enterprise Councils (TECs) actually came into being in 1989. Crowley-Bainton (1997), similar to many others, holds the view that TECs emerged as an affirmation of the ideology that supports '[t]he trend towards market-oriented training systems' which 'gives an increasingly prominent role to the private sector' and within which '[e]nterprises, in particular, are expected to undertake a proactive role in training' (p.1). TECs were in this context, therefore, the product of a drive to 'attract private sector involvement and promote enterprise culture' (Rowntree Foundation, 1998, p.2).

The priorities of TECs were to create and maintain dynamic and local economies, support competitive business and build a world-class work-force. It is in the drive towards achieving its third priority that TECs most impacted on education in general and adult literacy in particular. To start with, these priorities consign the value position driving this policy to the realm of instrumentalism. The aims were to achieve ends which were irrevocably linked to economic outcomes. Some of the steps taken by TECs towards the achievement of their third priority were the establishment of processes and procedures for investing in employee development and creating a structure for access to and delivery of education through a variety of programmes including Youth Training, Training for Work, NVQS and Modern Apprenticeship (Rowntree Foundation, 1998).

One of the more relevant implications of the creation of TECs was that the control of training was shifted from educationalists to industrialists and employers. As can be expected, the driving force behind most industrialists is profit making. In effect, therefore, education was ceded into the control of people who consider profit and monetary values as supreme. This in a way heralded the formal acknowledgement that education must be instrumental rather than intrinsic.

Another significant impact of the TECs and their worldview relates to the point raised in our discussion. In their adherence to the instrumental perception of education, TECs focused mainly on employment as the ultimate desired outcome for which education must be an instrument. Hence, education must be used to prepare adults for the world of work. The result is that one of the major focuses of TECs' programmes was to improve employability skills within the society. However, even this seemingly straightforward vision had some tension attached to it.

DOI: 10.1057/9781137535115.0003

In a research on training partnerships across Europe, Crowley-Bainton (1997) observes that there is a divergence of opinion between the various constituencies that make up the TECs. While the representatives of the Confederation of British Industries (CBI) 'believe that too much effort is expended on equipping the unemployed to return to work, rather than upskilling or reskilling existing workforces', the others consider the reverse to be the desired state. This divergence in opinion suggests that different groups within the TEC set-up were simply interested in driving forward agendas that favoured a return on the human capital invested. While the members representing the industry were more interested in making profit for the industry, those representing the government were more interested in cutting government's overhead dictated by the ethos of the welfare state in catering for the unemployed. Either way, the focus, we argue, is on returns to capital investment and, therefore, a reflection of a human capital value position.

Regardless of the seeming difference on which members of the society the capital must be spent on, there was an agreement on the desired outcomes, a focus on employment needs. It becomes inevitable, therefore, that the direct intrinsic needs of those to be trained paled into insignificance with the instrumental vision of the TEC stakeholders gaining ascendancy. The direct implication of this viewpoint was that vocalisation of education was firmly put into the agenda of educational practice and policy.

This position impacted significantly on the evolution of policy and practice in the field of adult education. At the level of policy, because a significant part of the funding for adult literacy was provided from the budget of TECs, literacy was located within the framework of employment, thus reinforcing the theme of vocalisation and, ultimately, instrumentalisation. Vocalisation in this context becomes an outcome to be achieved through the instrument of literacy. Putting this into perspective, Sir Brian Wolfson, the chair of the National Training Taskforce, in his address to the 1990 ALBSU conference noted that there must be a change in the outlook of both employers and literacy providers and that '[e]mployers should give priority to literacy and basic skills because they are the foundation of occupational competency' (ALBSU, 1990, p.1).

In the context of practice, one implication of the creation of TECs was the introduction of National Vocational Qualifications (NVQS). Enterprises played a leading role in devising the NVQs, which covered all occupation and sectors. NVQ competences are expressed in terms of

DOI: 10.1057/9781137535115.0003

a range of activities and the level of competence needed in order to be able to carry out particular tasks. They are, therefore, in essence a model for meeting key employment requirements presented as competences. This template impacted on the practice of literacy from the viewpoint of assessment and curriculum content. On the one hand, adult literacy began to borrow the competence framework for the assessment of learners. The focus was no longer on assessing learners' progress on the basis of their needs and personal goals, but on the basis of a set of competences that was mainly influenced by perceived employment needs. On the other hand, the curriculum itself was significantly shifted from learner-needs-led to employer-needs-led. In the field of adult literacy, therefore, as it has done in other educational fields, the new qualification brought occupations into the qualification framework and through this created a form of national framework, which hitherto did not exist.

There is no doubt that all of these developments are again a reflection of a shift towards a value position of instrumentalisation. Specific outcomes became attached to the study of literacy with these outcomes valued basically in terms of their economic significance, that value position thus links adult literacy to employment and economic returns. In essence, this is another phase in the movement of transition, a transition for an intrinsic value position to an instrumentalist value position.

Some comments from participants from a study referred to earlier demonstrate that this perception was widely held by practitioners. One interviewee notes that:

> you sort of get the feeling that you no longer had control over anything. What's even worse was that the students were left floundering and wondering what happened to their initial dreams.

Another interviewee said:

> if you wanted your classes to survive, you did what the TECs wanted your local funders to do, and that usually is to take away the individual dreams of your learners. It was all kind of geared towards this dream of vocationalising everything.

Essentially, therefore, the advent of TECs foregrounded the theme of vocationalisation in the context of the discourse of employment and competitiveness. All of these are again relevant within the larger discourse of international competitiveness and profitability for

DOI: 10.1057/9781137535115.0003

employers of labour. Education began to be seen not merely as an entitlement as it was under the welfarist ethos, but as a market commodity.
To reinforce this notion of education in general and adult literacy in
particular, the notions of standard and qualifications were reinforced.
These served as tools for controlling the content and mode of delivery
of adult literacy and were monitored through the deployment of a
funding mechanism.

The abolition of ILEA and the introduction of word- and numberpower in 1990

The abolition of ILEA

One of the fallouts of the ERA was the abolition of the ILEA. As with the
ERA itself, the significance of this event manifested more in its impact
than in the content of the act itself. Many commentators have observed
that the decision to abolish the ILEA was more political than educational. While arguing a case for what he sees as the erosion of democracy
through economic decisions, Lauder (1991, p.417) argues:

> The 'conviction politics' of Mrs Thatcher's period in office has brought the
> question of democracy to the fore. In education alone, there is a catalogue of
> examples where it could be argued, the spirit of democracy, if not the law, has
> been abused. To but four: the abolition of the ILEA, for political rather than
> educational reasons.

But it is not simply the motivation for embarking on this route that is of
importance here. More significant is the impact that this has on educational policy and practice in general and adult literacy policy and practice in particular. One acknowledgement of the impact of the abolition
is that made by Fowler (2005, p.16), who notes that 'it symbolised' what
she calls 'the end of a previous "Zeitgeist"'. 'Zeitgeist' refers to a political
ideology. She goes further, in concurrence with Fieldhouse et al. (1999),
to locate this in the contest of adult literacy asserting that:

> The abolition of ILEA can be seen to signify the removal of power from alter-
> native forms of education provision, and was particularly damaging for adult
> literacy provision and development. This is significant in the context of the
> fact that ILEA had been instrumental in promoting campaign events against
> illiteracy, and for setting up the Language and Literacy Unit (LLU) within
> which many liberal literacy ideologies thrived.

DOI: 10.1057/9781137535115.0003

This was essentially an impact on the ideological slant of literacy policy and practice, and there were further such significant impacts.

In the abstract to a research on active citizenship and adult learning in inner London, Payne (1990) presents the following findings, among others. First, he concludes that 'A generalised funding crisis in Inner London was found to be due to the abolition of ILEA and the implementation of the poll tax', and second that there was 'increasing emphasis on job and examination oriented courses' (Abstract, p.1). Drawing from these comments, we could conclude that the abolition of the ILEA simply helped in driving forward the agenda of vocalisation, which was prevalent in the context of the existing discourse of economy and employment. In this respect, therefore, this simply converges with government's ideology of skills rather than knowledge development and the desire to accommodate the demands of the industry. In addition, it signifies the continued regulation of funding, such that it could be used as an instrument for enforcing standards and for prescribing the content of what should count as literacy. This had particular significance for the practice of adult literacy, as it helped enforce the newly emerging test-centred culture in adult literacy which anchors the instrumentalist and human capital value positions that now drive literacy policy and practice.

Perhaps the most significant implication for adult literacy is the fact that it signalled a form of decentralisation, which naturally initiated a process of closer control. As with the ERA, the abolition of the ILEA was essentially the creation of a new formula for power relations. While the former transferred power from local to central government, the latter devolved control from a higher to a lower tier of government. In effect, adult literacy provisions became structured in a way that permitted closer monitoring and became subject to a number of prescriptive regimes. Those prescriptions, we argue, were essentially about expected outcomes. Adult literacy became conceived as an instrument for achieving these outcomes.

As with many of the other significant events, the themes of standardisation, often represented by the imposition of an assessment regime and the replacement of knowledge drive with skill drive, were very prominent in the evolution of both policy and practice in the field of adult literacy. It is, however, significant to note that both these were geared towards the achievement of the agenda of vocationalisation. The overarching theme, therefore, could be seen as vocationalisation of education with funding

DOI: 10.1057/9781137535115.0003

control and assessment serving as tools for achieving this goal. This is a view shared by experienced practitioners. One described the situation aptly noting,

> We all suddenly found ourselves working to agendas that we knew nothing of, and this thing about qualifications and lack of funding, which presumably, were impacts of this abolition of the ILEA simply kind of swamped us.

Another commented,

> It was obvious, at least to some of us, that the government was consumed by this thing about improving skills, reducing unemployment, and so on, because they had this deficit view of literacy. The new LEAS, who inherited the role of the ILEA, appeared to be driving forward this agenda.

The introduction of standardised assessment: wordpower and numberpower

Another significant policy movement/event in the evolution of adult literacy policy and practice is the introduction of a standardised assessment regime through the word and number power awards. Wordpower and Numberpower assessment systems were essentially the first set of assessment to be accorded the status of a 'national accreditation for adult basic education learners' (Hamilton and Merrifield, 2000, p.3; Brooks, 2007, p.3). This suggests that this system of assessment provided a template upon which assessment in the field of adult literacy was built. Taking the lead roles in the development of this assessment system were the MSC and ALBSU, both of which were government agencies. Although the two agencies ostensibly collaborated in the development of the assessment system, there is some evidence that this was an uneasy relationship, and that, in fact, the MSC took a lead role. The MSC with its larger funding clout was, as one practitioner puts it, 'in the driving seat' though ALBSU remained the official face of ALLN, taking up 'good practice' and proselytising it in the field through its training events, special development projects and a series of high-quality publications.

What this suggests is that the assessment system itself was subsumed within the framework of the ethos of skills and vocationalisation, which informed a substantial proportion of the work of the MSC. This again is another evidence of the movement of adult literacy towards an instrumental value position. On the one hand, assessment itself became the

DOI: 10.1057/9781137535115.0003

desired outcome of literacy learning; on the other hand, success in the assessment activities was seen as the achievement of the goal of vocationalisation and skill development.

Although this assessment system, on the face of it, was developed in response to the existing informal approaches to assessment, it would seem that the main objective was to respond to 'the need for ALLN to be incorporated into the national framework for vocational qualifications' (Hamilton and Hillier, 2007, p.584). But as noted by Hillier (2006) these qualification systems simply added to the qualifications jungle whilst critically changing the culture and practices of ALLN. Further insight into this argument is provided in a study carried out by Hamilton and Hillier (2007, p.584) in which a practitioner commented,

> There was a very big change across most basic skills work with the advent of Wordpower and Numberpower and with that move to competence based work. Everyone was thinking competency and NVQs based assessments, everybody was developing assignments. The sense of group and creativity got lost except with oldies who had been there whilst it was still crackling and with people who had been trained in that way.

What this confirms is the fact that the real impact of the introduction of this system of assessment was the introduction of competence-based assessment and the concretisation of the vocalisation agenda in the field of adult literacy through an assessment regime. Overall, these reflect the features of an instrumentalist value position. There are specific assessment outcomes associated with literacy studies and beyond that, there are ultimate outcomes which are associated with the achievement of employment and economic goals.

It is important to locate this development in the context of the overarching discourses of unemployment, economy and the proscribed government remedy of vocationalisation of education. Hamilton and Hillier (2007, p.580) identified the enabling environment for this development, particularly with the role of the MSC and its successor body, the Training Agency (TA). They note that:

> With increasing unemployment, the Manpower Services Commission (MSC) and its successor body, the Training Agency, responsible for vocational preparation and training became much more heavily involved with ALLN and brought its own approach to assessment. Major awarding bodies, the Royal Society of Arts (RSA) and City and Guilds, offered qualifications in language, communication skills and numeracy.

DOI: 10.1057/9781137535115.0003

But this was merely a precursor to the standardised national award which was embodied in the creation of the Wordpower and Numberpower assessment system. We may note that this move was robustly opposed by both learners and practitioners in the field. Indeed, the FEFC (1998) appears to acknowledge the reluctance of learners to embrace the assessment regime that was imposed by the introduction of Wordpower, if only partially, noting that:

> Some students, however, still do not perceive accreditation to be of value, given their immediate circumstances, and some teachers do not offer students sufficient encouragement to register for qualifications.

This suggests that the issue of gaining qualifications, which can be seen as an indicator of achieving competence, is very important to the FEFC who were at the time the funders of adult literacy education. But by far more insightful are the comments of many practitioners as presented in a report by Hamilton (2005). One tutor commented:

> I remember introducing the idea of the open college passport and being able to build up credits and adult students getting certification for work and, explaining for that to happen, we were going to have to keep some records. And it caused complete consternation.

Another noted:

> So if you were doing a basic skills class in literacy and numeracy you had to do Numberpower or Wordpower and the adults didn't want to do Numberpower and Wordpower, they hated it. We didn't like delivering it and they didn't like doing it but it was the only way of getting funding through the local authority.

The introduction of Wordpower accreditation in the field of adult literacy had one crucial impact: it helped to reinforce the theme of standardisation, which manifested itself in the form of a one-size-fits-all form of assessment. Because providers were compelled to register their learners for this award, it became inevitable that the curriculum would be influenced by the assessment regime. Teachers were compelled to teach to the assessment requirement rather than to meet the needs of their learners. In this sense, practice in the field began to lose its student-centred approach and more importantly helped to entrench the instrumental ethos that was gradually taking over the entirety of adult literacy policy and practice.

DOI: 10.1057/9781137535115.0003

Helping to impose the assessment-driven standard was the intro-duction of another element of funding control. Providers were able to draw funds only if they demonstrated evidence of putting their learners through the Wordpower accreditation requirements. This had implica-tions for policy from the viewpoint that there was now an official position which stipulated, that only courses that met these conditions could be funded. This development echoes the human capital value position. The value associated with literacy was located in assessment outcome which is itself seen as evidence to well-spent capital. Assessment, therefore, was not just an end, but also a means to an end.

But by far more important is the fact that the introduction of this assessment framework helped to formalise the process of integrating literacy into a vocational framework. The assessment requirements, which were competence based, and which reflected the substantial input of the MSC/TA, provided the opportunity to vocationalise literacy provi-sions. In effect, therefore, the then newly introduced assessment regime provided a base for the convergence of literacy and vocational studies and clearly manifested the instrumental value position of adult literacy policy and practice.

From the ongoing, it becomes obvious that the introduction of the Wordpower assessment system was in reality a tool for promoting the value positions of vocationalisation, employment and the economy, all of which derive their relevance from the context of the prevalent discourse of economic management, competitiveness and vocationalisation as a remedy for unemployment.

The Further and Higher Education Act and the Creation of the Further Education Funding Council, 1992

The Further and Higher Education Act of 1992 (henceforth FHE act) and the attendant creation of the Further Education Funding Council has often been described by scholars in the field as the single most important event in the evolution of adult education policy and practice in the 1990s. In no other sphere of further education is this perception truer than in the field of adult literacy policy and practice. The importance of this act, in our view, is located in its role as the lynchpin in the dispensation of a

DOI: 10.1057/9781137535115.0003

political ideology that has since affected every sphere of the educational system in the United Kingdom to date.

Let us see some of the opinions relevant people hold about it. In a lecture given at the University of East London, Alan Tucket, the then director of the National Institute for Adult and Continuing Education (NIACE), captures the political relevance of the act when he declares:

> The Further and Higher Education Act was, perhaps, the high-water mark of the drive towards utilitarianism in education policy-certainly as far as it impacted on adult learners. Spurred on by arguments developed by Sheila Lawlor, who argued that all local education spending on adult education was in theft of resources which ought to be spent on schools, the then government prepared a white paper whose early draft suggested a ban on funding uncertified adult education except between consenting adults in areas of extreme disadvantage, when funding should be covered by social services budget. (2001,p.2)

Within the structure of this proposal, two issues emerge immediately. First is the notion of enforced consent, which suggests that the adults to be funded must agree to some conditions before benefiting from the available funding. The second issue arising from the proposal is the de-prioritisation of adult education and a perception that the promotion of adult education must be subject to state benevolence under the social services. Thus, the underpinning value of the FHE act was essentially a political ideology, which embraces a value position that rates the importance of adult education only in terms of its economic relevance.

In the implementation of the act, perhaps, the two of the most significant elements were the incorporation of colleges and the establishment of the FEFC. Linked to these was the creation of the infamous 'schedule two' provision, which identified programmes that can be funded under adult education by the new funding body, FEFC. The introduction of schedule two meant that adult education was no longer a right, but a service, the provision of which was subject to a process of selection. Selection itself was a function of economic values. As noted by Tucket (p.4),

> Given tight budgets for public investment (and in the UK this was the era of Mrs. Thatcher and the belief in the flawless efficiency of markets), there was an understandable desire to give priority to spending on areas which seemed likely to make the maximum impact on labour market performance.

Thus, the themes of competitiveness and market economy were again very significant in both the proposal and implementation of the FHE act.

DOI: 10.1057/9781137535115.0003

In the context of adult literacy, these developments had a huge impact on the evolution of practice and policy. Hamilton and Hillier (2006) are emphatic in their argument that:

> it was the Further and Higher Education Act that most affected the future shape of ALLN. The importance of the act derives more from its repercussions than from the act itself. In the first place, the incorporation of colleges, which was one of the fallouts of the act, meant that, in the words of Hamilton and Hillier ... 'The colleges became incorporated businesses, responsible for their own financial affairs, and an era of competition arose between providers, as they were encouraged to increase student numbers, but with a reduction in the unit funding'. (p.12)

In a political setting where the utilitarian ideology was the order of the day in the field of education, incorporated businesses, as colleges had become, turned into a major tool in the implementation of policy. The response to the act in the field of adult literacy was a frenzied rush to get adult literacy on the schedule two list. Indeed, getting on the list was a product of intense lobbying. Tucket (2001, p.2) noted that even tutors connived in this by 'turning poorly funded uncertificated work into accredited, and, therefore, better financed "schedule two" provision'. The effect was that older learners, whose rationales for embarking on these courses were more intrinsic than instrumental, simply abandoned them. Tucket further notes that this had significant adverse effect on adult literacy as 'Between 1991 and 1994 NIACE mapped a 40% fall in older learners' participation'. In effect, many adults who really desired and needed adult literacy were excluded by the advent of the FHE act.

The FHE act impacted on adult literacy practice in a number of ways. First, it signalled the final step in the vocationalisation of literacy provision. Because of the need for funding, many providers were forced to structure their courses in a way that would meet the vocational structure prevalent in colleges. Second, most of the literacy provision migrated into FE colleges, as they were the ones predominantly funded by the FEFC. The direct impact of this was that adult literacy provision became a business venture as the providers had themselves effectively become businesses since incorporation. The third direct impact was the emergence of a central monitoring and inspectorate regime, which was driven by funding control. As the FEFC now hold the purse string, they had the wherewithal to impose their (government's) perception of literacy, which was geared towards upskilling and vocationalisation. This brought with

DOI: 10.1057/9781137535115.0003

it the attendant elements of standardisation and accreditation, as conditions for funding required that specific contents were delivered and that every funded provision had an assessment outcome. Overall, the FHE act became an enabling tool for the government to impose tighter control on the provision of adult literacy and for finally shifting the focus from meeting the needs of individuals to meeting the economic needs of the state. In the course of doing this, adult literacy was forced to change its value position from an intrinsic one to an instrumental one.

There is no doubt that the driving forces behind these changes were the dominant themes of vocationalism, economic competitiveness and employment. It could also be argued that the act was a conscious response by the government to problems in the economy and the labour market. Bradley (1997), in his analysis of the impact of the FHE act using a neo-Marxian analysis, shows how the act was used to steer adult education policy solely towards vocational qualifications. The inherent argument is that the act was in itself a form of state reaction to the perception of a changing employment market. Presenting a similar argument, Tucket (2001) locates the act in a wider European context. He argues that:

> governments throughout the industrialised world were reacting to changes in technology that collapsed the boundaries of established industrialised disciplines; to the decline of unskilled work and the growth of knowledge-rich work. (pp.2–3)

The FHE act could, therefore, be seen as the tool for responding to economic and labour problems through the replacement of liberal/intrinsic education value position with a new right value position of utilitarianism.

DOI: 10.1057/9781137535115.0003

3

The Consolidation of an Instrumental Value Position: The Moser Committee

Abstract: *This chapter draws on empirical research, which includes rich data from interviews with members of a policy development committee to identify the underpinning value positions that drove the Moser Report, one of the major policy initiatives in the field of adult literacy in the past decade. Moving from the central Skills for Life (SfL) policy to previous and subsequent policies, we argue that this period saw the consolidation of the influence of the instrumental/human capital value position in adult literacy. Literacy is thus expressed, for example, as 'functional' skills and driven by the premise of a 'knowledge economy'. Within this philosophical stance one of the most significant duties given to education is to provide a flexible, adaptable and skilled workforce to make countries competitive in the globalised economy. It focuses on education for work positions and education as a commodity and pays no regard to issues of economic, political and social equality.*

Keywords: adult literacy; empirical data; instrumental and human capital; policy; value positions

Ade-Ojo, Gordon and Vicky Duckworth. *Adult Literacy Policy and Practice: From Intrinsic Values to Instrumentalism.* Basingstoke: Palgrave Macmillan, 2015. DOI: 10.1057/9781137535115.0004.

In this chapter, we argue that the value position of instrumentalism/ human capital that had been evolving and gradually dominating policy and practice in adult literacy education became fully entrenched with the recommendations of the Moser Committee and the attendant policies it generated. However, our approach to the analysis here draws more significantly from empirical data which were collected through interviews with members of the Moser Committee. It was possible for us to take this approach because of the relative currency of the period and the policy driver. This meant that we were able to access some of those who contributed to policy and the attendant practice dictates. In discussing the findings from our interviews, similar patterns, as well as emerging themes, sometimes divergent on the same issue, are identified. Arguments are then put forward on the basis of the identified themes and pattern to support claims about the dominant value position that was responsible for the shape and direction of adult literacy practice and policy, as manifested in the SFL policy.

The composition of the committee appears to be a good starting point in our exploration of policy at this stage. There are a number of reasons for seeking this information. First, we anticipate that it will help to answer the following relevant questions: (1) did the respondents see their membership as a product of their experience in the field of adult literacy, or indeed, adult education? (2) What do the members feel that they were able to contribute to the task on the basis of their experience? (3) Furthermore, the question aimed to find out if members saw themselves as representatives of particular sectors or ideological viewpoint.

These issues are important as they might help in establishing the source of the value positions that might be at play in the evolution of policy.

Summary of findings

Overall, there were divergent views by the members on the relevance of their experience to the task of policy development in the area of adult literacy. While some members were convinced that their experience and background had prepared them for this role, others felt that very few members of the committee had any serious experience in the field of adult literacy that could have prepared them for the role. The latter, while willing to acknowledge the need for experience and skills from

DOI: 10.1057/9781137535115.0004

other areas, felt that the nature of the experiences that were brought to the committee were not particularly relevant to the practice of adult literacy. The membership of the committee included representatives from the civil service, the industry, and economic experts.

A summary of the specific experience brought to the committee included the experience of contributing to the process of prioritising basic skills for employability, experience of functioning within the structure of a monitoring agency, experience of working in workforce employment, research experience in a number of areas including the relationship between basic skills and employment, economics and statistics, limited experience as a practitioner although only in a related field and a long time before being involved in this role, experience of managing a portfolio in which vocational training was very important, Trade union activities with some focus on the job training.

In our view, the composition of this committee signalled the ultimate goal of the government from the onset. There is a predominance of members who had previously done work relating to employment and employability. In contrast, there was only one person within the main committee, who had some experience of working in an area close to adult literacy and this was decades before the committee was set up. In our view, the composition of the committee provides an indication that there is an inclination towards policies that accommodate employment or at least acknowledge it. A typical description of the previous experience of the members of the committee is shown here:

> I am not an educationalist though I actually spent a great bulk of my career, and indeed spent the rest of it in – largely in education, educational training and employment.

This, for us, echoes the value position of instrumentalism that had become dominant in the previous period. But what were the views of the committee members about its composition?

Many of the members interviewed were convinced that their previous experiences had adequately prepared them for the task of contributing to the development of adult literacy policy. However, a minority of members interviewed felt that the range of experience represented in the committee was simply not adequate. This raises a very fundamental question. What really was the perception of the members in terms of the task to be accomplished? What was their perception of the nature of the policy that was to be developed? These questions become even

DOI: 10.1057/9781137535115.0004

more pertinent in the context of the predominance of members with experience of work, vocation and employment issues. In the perception of the minority, there was a pronounced representation of members with a pedigree of prioritising employment.

What emerged from the perception of members in terms of their experience is the common thread that they mostly had some form of experience in areas related to employment. This suggests that while it is true that many of the members were highly experienced in the areas of work-related training and employment, there was a very limited relationship to the field of adult literacy practice. We might, therefore, deduce that the perception of themselves as 'highly experienced' brings into question the goals that needed to be achieved. Were these goals purely related to adult literacy in its intrinsic form, or were they contingent on the issue of employment? As indicated, there was a minority and a majority view to this question.

The differing points of view expressed by respondents suggest that the perception of the 'self' might have been coloured by the expectation of individuals within the committee in terms of what they hoped to contribute and what their perception of what is expected of them might be. Although it was quite evident that most members had the perception that they had very limited experience of administering or teaching literacy, most felt that the experience they had, which was predominantly related to employment and training, was highly relevant. This gives an indication that for most of the members of the committee, although the nodal discourse pervading the policy development was adult literacy, the major theme underlying it was actually employment and training. In this respect, therefore, it is logical for them to hold a perception of their range of experience as highly relevant to the process of policy development in the field of adult literacy.

Without question, the general position regarding relevance suggests that there is a continuation of the drive towards re-skilling, ameliorating what was perceived as dire employment/unemployment figures and the attempt to vocationalise education at the post-compulsory level. In our view, this simply provides a basis for the claim that there might have been some form of political and ideological perception that, from the onset, coloured the vision of the task placed before the committee. In this respect, there might have been the suggestion that the deliberations of the committee was not expected to centre on adult literacy as an intrinsic variable but as an instrumental educational endeavour.

DOI: 10.1057/9781137535115.0004

In the case of the adult literacy policy development, the evidence emanating from the views of members of the committee in terms of their perceptions of the relevance of their experience suggests that these pressures were informed by the themes of employment, training and skills. As a result, while most members acknowledge their limitation in the field of literacy, they remained adamant that their experience in the field of employment and workforce training was not only required, but also highly sufficient for the task to be executed. We could, therefore, argue that there is some evidence deriving from the expectations of members that the driving value position for this policy base was an instrumental one.

At the interview, we further sought to establish the perception of the individual members of the committee of the importance of the whole group composition. The rationale for this was to find out if there were perceptions of a pre-determined agenda on the basis of the composition. In addition, it is expected that this focus might bring to light the expectations of individuals on what others within the committee might contribute to the process. Did individual members have a perception that others were in the committee for a particular purpose? Did they have the perception that the overall composition was suitable for executing the task at hand? Did they have the perception that the composition of the group had implications for the outcomes on the basis of the individual and combined socio-cognitive realities? These were some of the issues that this interview focus was expected to resolve. It is important, however, to highlight the difference between this interview focus and that of the first focus analysed earlier. While the first interview focus wanted the views of individuals on themselves, the second focus wanted the views of individuals on the group. In essence, the difference can be surmised as that between individual assessment of self as against individual assessment of group.

Views on group formation can be broadly classified into two categories: positive and negative perceptions. In the case of those whose perception of the composition is described as positive, there was a general view that the composition of the group reflected a degree of competence and that members were included simply on the basis of their ability to deliver a viable policy for literacy. But sharply contrasting with this view were responses which suggested that the composition of the group might in fact have some deep-rooted significance. Some key views expressed within this sub-group included too many members

DOI: 10.1057/9781137535115.0004

knew too little of the subject area of adult literacy; the composition reflected a power dynamics which favoured members with some form of economic background; there was key representation of members of the industry in the composition of the group; there was an obvious lack of representation of practitioners in the composition of the group; there was a pattern of ideological linkage among some members of the group, which manifested significantly in the predominance of members with leaning towards labour and employment.

The conflicting perceptions on the composition of the committee reflected, in a way, what might be seen as the divergent ideological leanings of the members. It is, therefore, not surprising that while some saw it in a positive light, others saw it in a negative light. For example, while those who held a positive perception argued that the predominance of labour-and economics-value-inclined members was necessary, and indeed an advantage in terms of negotiating with government, there is another possible explanation for this configuration. In the first place, it could be argued that the pre-eminence of labour and economics value proponents in the committee signified the fact that the agenda of the committee was to be driven by the government's economic policy and the lingering move towards skills and vocationalisation, and that this position would be aptly represented and argued by these members within the committee. This would fit into the framework for describing the New Labour educational policy, which focuses predominantly on up-skilling and vocationalisation (Allen and Ainley, 2007) and, therefore, draws from an instrumental value position. The divergence in the import of this pattern of composition can be captured by the following quotes from different respondents. While describing some members of the committee in terms of their relevance and the role played within the committee, one respondent declared: 'knows absolutely nothing about this area, yet he felt perfectly confident to pronounce and decide and actually hold enormous sway, because, of course, he is a big man in the world'. Given this possible scenario, one could argue that the prevalent government arguments and policies on employment, labour and the economy were simply handed down to the committee by proxy.

While the preceding arguments relate to responses from members of the committee who saw the composition of the working group in a negative light, responses from those who perceived it positively also provide some insight into how the composition of the panel might have been value laden. One such respondent, while making claims that the committee in his view 'was balanced', went on to conclude that the 'different perspectives were all equal'. What this respondent overlooked, however, was the fact he was only able to list members from the private sector and government representatives from monitoring agencies like the BSA. Indeed, this respondent opined that his preference would have been to have 'heard more from the private sector as we were a bit sort of supply led rather than demand led'. This statement provides a glimpse of the economic argument, which would prefer to model the shaping of educational policy and practice after the Human Capital value position.

O'Keefe (1999, pp.19–20) sheds some light on this line of thinking when arguing a case for a linkage between markets, knowledge and ideology. He opines that 'markets are not single conscious minds but aggregations of separate individual intelligences' and that this forms a basis for the argument that 'the market economy is a better knowledge system … coordinating the available knowledge far more efficiently and comprehensively that any government agency could'.

Thus, we have an insight into the possible thinking behind the composition of the committee and the lop-sided slant towards economic and employment issue experts. The thinking, in line with O'Keefe's argument (p.20), might well be to introduce separate individual intelligences, which is, in this case, conditioned by an absolute trust in the viability and efficiency of the market economy. This, one could argue, would guarantee that the government's preferred value position of instrumentalism would be pushed to the fore.

One emergent issue for us was the possibility of putting people on the committee whose views were already known and who the government was confident would carry out its agenda. This raises the sceptre of the twin factors of pre-determination and the overarching government value position of instrumentalist/economy-driven educational policy. One member sheds some more light on the possible reasoning behind the inclusion of particular members in the committee. For this member, the real purpose of the committee was entirely different from the superficial purpose of drawing up policy for adult literacy. He reminded us that 'What it was for is to effectively persuade the treasury to spend large sums of public money on supporting remedial literacy and numeracy'. In this member's view, this task is not one for educationalists, as it entails 'presenting them with the argument about why it is good for the economy and the labour market', and, it is not one 'for an FE teacher from somewhere' to carry out. The real issue surreptitiously emerging here might be

DOI: 10.1057/9781137535115.0004

that there has been a pre-determination of what the committee needed to achieve and one way of guaranteeing that it was through the nature of its composition. As indicated by the respondent cited, the government needed people who could convincingly argue an economic and labour market case. We argue, therefore, that the committee's composition reflects this ultimate goal.

From the viewpoint of education in a general sense, Pring (2005, p.429) gives an indication of what might be the driving factors behind the educational policy of the period in question, and which in his view have remained the influential factors in the educational policy direction of New Labour. While arguing that education itself appears to have no place in the goals of most policies, he concludes that the main reason is because policy is often:

> trapped in language which militates against the broader moral dimension of education – the language of skills and targets, of performance indicators and audits, of academic studies and vocational pathways, of economic relevance and social usefulness.

If indeed these were the guiding principles underpinning the evolution of policy, and if as suggested the composition was configured in order to push a pre-determined government agenda through, we could put forward the following argument: the driving factors in the evolution of adult literacy and practice from the viewpoint of the composition of the committee were the themes of economy, vocationalism and employment, as embodied in the notion of social usefulness and accountability, all of which are encapsulated in the value positions of instrumentalism and human capital.

The government's mandate to the working group

We sought the views of the committee members regarding the mandate given to the committee by the government because we wanted to see if we could gain some insight into the government's goals and thinking. Our assumption was that the dominant value position that informed the thinking of the government in the area of adult literacy was likely to be revealed or at least reflected through the mandate offered to the committee. A number of questions arise here. Was the mandate such that it would allow the working group to identify the existing problem

DOI: 10.1057/9781137535115.0004

and proffer solutions? Was it of a nature that it would be constrained to proffer solutions to an already identified and defined problem? These are important questions because answers to them would offer insight into how the problem was defined and the boundaries within which the committee was allowed to operate. Thus, the rationale for this interview was to clarify whether the mandate came to the committee in an un-allured form, or if it came enrobed in an already identified value position. If the latter were the case, it would then be possible to identify what the value positions were and as such identify them as influential factors in the outcomes of the work of the committee.

The responses of interviewees reflect differences along two lines. On the one hand, there was an evident difference in views regarding whether or not there was any mandate given to the committee. On the other hand, there were differences, even among those who agreed that there was a mandate, on what the mandate was and its nature. The views held amongst the members of the committee can be summarised as follows.

1 The problem was already identified and there was an indirect mandate to provide solution to the identified mandate.
2 The problem that was identified was presented with a preferred solution and the real mandate of the committee was to give a public seal of approval to the solution.
3 The government's own preferred value position, instrumental education, which has a central goal of promoting employment and giving financial accountability was at the heart of the mandate.

Illustrating this view is the response by one member:

> the mandate was for the first time ever, to be reduced to a national strategy regarding the development of basic skills...and then sort of position basic skills very very strongly in terms of the government's agenda and priority.

A similar opinion held by some members of the committee was that while the government had already identified the problem, the mandate was to define, quantify and legitimise the problem through a statistical approach. For those who held this view, the central plank on which their evidence was built was the fact that ready-made information from specific sources was kind of imposed on the committee for its use. As such, there is a suggestion that there was little room for manoeuvre in terms of the interpretation of these documents

DOI: 10.1057/9781137535115.0004

and in terms of the decisions that the committee was able to make on a number of issues. A member who held this view puts this into perspective when he noted that:

> the evidence that we had for this, for this piece of work, ... I always thought was quite thin. ... the various bodies that were around and were providing us with free data research ... and we didn't carry out or commission the research ourselves, we were writing strategies on the basis of evidence that had been previously provided, possibly in some cases, for a different purpose.

Another view strongly held by members of the committee was that the mandate was embodied in the chair, representatives of the BSA and a few members who were close to the chair literally and ideologically. This type of viewpoint leaves us in the realm of inferences and conjectures. Even if this was the situation within the committee, a crucial question is how we ascertain what the ideological leaning of the chairman and his 'acolytes' was. We can probably hazard a guess based on the pedigree of the chairman and some of the other members who worked closely with him. The limited evidence we have leads us to classify the inclination of these members of the committee as belonging to the human capital tradition. In previous and subsequent public pronouncements, they have offered the economic argument in the calculation of educational value. On the basis of this, we make the claim that an instrumental value position might be at play through a pre-determined agenda. We accept that this is a rather tenuous claim but expect that corroboration of the position we have taken here might be provided through other areas we investigated. Some comments from members which suggest the possibility of a pre-determined agenda that draws from an instrumental value position include:

> 'We worked through an agenda that was, I think, determined between the basic skills agency and *'. Let's face it, I think there was an agenda which said an awful lot of work has gone in this area, in teaching, which isn't much good and it is sloppy and it's too cosy and it doesn't produce measurable outcomes through testing, and the whole thing needs overhauling.

And,

> My feeling was that it was the topics that were going to be discussed were fairly prescribed ... The framing of the agendas were with the chair. I mean the chair was very much in control, despite ... he was nevertheless in charge, and in control, and holding the things from beginning to end.

DOI: 10.1057/9781137535115.0004

Another view held by a minority of members was that the mandate was implied and defined and that it centred on how the policy might address wealth creation by raising skills levels. Illustrating this position are the following responses from some members of the committee:

> Yes, the mandate had two components. One was, you might say, wealth creation, improving the economy by raising skills levels in the population which an international survey had suggested were very much lower in Britain than in other European countries.

And,

> There was no doubt that one of the main line the committee wanted to think about was the impact that improved basic skills could have economically and essentially that means in terms of getting people – either getting them – so they are participating in the world of work.

If the opinions expressed in the two comments were correct, we again have evidence that the agenda was not only pre-determined, but also informed by an instrumental value position. From the first comment it was clear that in the view of this member, the goal for which literacy was an instrument is wealth creation. From the second comment, there is an indication of the view that the central driver was the ultimate goal of getting people to participate in the world of employment.

A different perception was, however, provided through another minority view, which suggests that the mandate was to use the policy to ameliorate social exclusion. Some of the members who expressed this opinion felt that the government's agenda, and ultimately, the committee's agenda were driven by the theme of social inclusion. This view is captured in the following response:

> I mean there were some wider sets of principles about social inclusion and employability, the government's approach to widening access. I mean the Kennedy Report on wider participation was quite dominant to that point.

This view surprisingly takes a departure from the dominant value position of human capital. On one level, it might be argued that this was a slight shift towards the intrinsic value position, as the element of social inclusion might suggest that the value of literacy for inclusion is not necessarily economic in orientation. Nonetheless, the element of instrumentalism remains in place, as literacy, even from this position, is seen as an instrument to be used by the government to achieve an identified and specific goal.

DOI: 10.1057/9781137535115.0004

The agenda of the committee

Generally, there were a number of commonalities in the positions taken by various respondents, which might suggest that the nature of the agenda could provide an insight into the most influential factors in the development of adult literacy policy by the Moser Committee. Contrasting positions in the perception of respondents are manifested in their views about what ideological argument informed the government's mandate and the agenda of the committee. While one view saw it as something informed by the notion of social inclusion and empowerment, the other view within the committee saw it as something informed by the themes of employment and the economy. What is, however, significant is the convergence of opinions in terms of what social features within which both viewpoints might be manifested. For those who saw the agenda as driven by an inclination towards widening participation and social inclusion, the evidence relied heavily on the employment and economic situations of the proposed beneficiaries of this policy. A similar indication is given in respect of the view that employability and economic considerations were the driving forces behind the agenda. As such, for both viewpoints, employment and the economy were projected as the important indices of both the current state and the projected position in relation to the arguments of each side.

The convergence of perception as highlighted, which is concretised in the importance of employment and economic factors, suggests that these two themes were particularly important in the shaping of the committee's agenda, and by direct implication, the evolution of adult literacy policy through the Moser Committee. They not only reflect the socio-cognitive reality of the government, but could also be seen as informing the socio-cognitive themes brought into play by members of the committee. It is to be expected, therefore, that whatever policy is generated by the committee will be concerned with addressing issues related to, or perceived through, the prism of economics and the labour market. In essence, therefore, we can argue that the central value position that drove the adult literacy policy and, therefore, practice is the instrumental/human capital value position.

But this simply confirms arguments that have been offered in terms of the overall direction of educational policy since the advent of the current New Labour government. As Allen and Ainley (2007) argue,

DOI: 10.1057/9781137535115.0004

debate about education policy has been part of a more general debate about how best to respond to these 'new times'. The 'new times' to which educational policies and practice are geared to respond to centre on the assumption that governments 'can no longer guarantee full employment or the traditional forms of welfare provision'. (p.21)

The response, therefore, is to ensure that educational policies can be acceptable only if they guaranteed that the outlay would help reduce the welfare burden of the state. Presumably, one way of doing this is to ensure that policy is informed by economic and labour market factors. This rationale is symbolised by the conclusions of the OECD (1988) on the future of social protection that 'Education and training are thus likely to become one of the main pillars of social security for tomorrow's citizens' (p.21).

Thus, we are offered some evidence that the pre-determined agenda that was given to the Moser Committee was itself a by-product of the value position that sees education as a remedy for social and economic ailments in the society, a perception that would necessarily attract a structure of literacy that would demand that it has a correlation with established measurable outputs, and which sees every form of learning as a step towards increasing a nation's stock of human capital such that their employability could be developed through education, thus facilitating the convergence of educational and economic policies within one systemic and ideological structure.

Views on tools used by the committee for collection of OECD data

The goal of this interview was to establish the views of members on the tool used for identifying the literacy problem, and which presumably sparked off the drive for a new adult literacy policy. The rationale for wanting to collect this information is tied to two arguments. First, there is the need to establish the extent to which the perception of the data collecting tool coloured the recommendations of members and, therefore, their recommendations. Second, this line of questioning, it was anticipated, would enable us to make deductions about the value position underpinning the structure of the tool. As an assessment and evaluation tool, it is inevitable that it would be conditioned by a worldview of education particularly in relation to what constitutes education.

DOI: 10.1057/9781137535115.0004

In addition, we felt that the acceptance or rejection of particular tools might give an indication of the influence that members' own value positions might have on their decision making. Therefore, while the findings from this line of questioning might not produce any conclusions on their own, they are expected to provide opportunities for making logical inferences and deductions.

The central tool used for the collection of the data was the OECD survey, although interestingly, many members did not know how exactly the tool was used and how it works. As with other interview foci, there were divergent opinions about the tools used in collecting the data that informed the work of the committee. While some were neutral, others were decidedly negative, and others still, relatively positive. A summary of all the viewpoints is presented in the paragraphs that follow.

In reality, only one finding could be seen as explicitly providing any kind of indication of the influence of a value position from this perspective. This finding was the acknowledgement of a few members that the tool focused only on a particular form of literacy practice. For members who held this view, the focus of the tool was on the traditional, testable form of literacy which is sometimes referred to as the autonomous model of literacy (Street, 1984). There is an abundance of studies in the literature that has linked this form of literacy to both the human capital and instrumental value positions (see, e.g., Gee, 1992; Street, 1984; Ade-Ojo, 2011). In effect, though not directly expressed, there is an implicit connection between the tool and the human capital/instrumental value positions.

Other findings with both negative and positive outlooks did not present explicit evidence on the possible influence of a value position. Nonetheless, we list some of them here and follow up by trying to tease out the implicit relationships between these findings and a dominant value position. Here is a summary of the findings:

1   There is the possibility that the tool and the information it presented might not be accurate.
2   There is a strong international comparative dimension associated with the tool and its findings.
3   There were concerns about the data collected through the use of the tool and particularly about the extrapolations drawn from the data.
4   Some members did not have any idea about the tool that was utilised in collecting the data that served as the basis for the committee's work.

DOI: 10.1057/9781137535115.0004

5 Although members who were aware of the tool knew that the result was untested and unverified, they were still willing to accept it as '100% gold carat'.

6 There was no debate around the adequacy of the tool and the legitimacy of its end product.

7 A few members felt that the tool was designed to measure what people could not do and conveniently ignores what they could do.

On a positive note, some members considered the tool as very reliable with some arguing that the tool was useful in presenting what interested many members of the committee.

Although with less than explicit relevance in terms of shedding light on our concern in this section, we could still conclude that the aggregation of responses provided by members of the committee interviewed suggest that the accuracy of the data collated through the OECD survey and which formed the basis of the committee's work might not be totally accurate. In addition, some respondents held the view that the tool itself was designed in a way to tease out only a particular type of information. In this respect, it was designed to tease out literacy competence based on a particular perception of literacy. In spite of this, however, the members were largely happy to go along with it and to make their recommendations on this basis. This raises a number of possibilities that are worth considering. We admit that the link we are about to make is extremely tenuous at best. Yet, we feel that it is important in terms of starting a process of thinking around how what might be seen on the surface of it as innocuous can sometimes be very important.

The views expressed about the tool raise the possibility of a potential convergence between the image of levels of literacy in the society reflected in the data and the perception held by members of the committee on what the literacy should be. If this was the case, we are again open to the possibility of a pre-determined agenda. As we have discussed earlier, some members suggested that the pre-determined agenda was driven by a human capital/instrumental value position. By agreeing with a questionable set of data that was foisted on the committee by the government and its agents, there is an indication that many members of the committee, at least all those who simply refuse to question the validity of the data presented, share the government's vision in terms of the role and goal of literacy. As has been argued earlier, the vision of the government at this time was essentially driven

DOI: 10.1057/9781137535115.0004

by economic and labour market issues. Following from this, we could infer that members who were compliant and who refused to challenge the validity of this data hold views that recognise the labour market and the economy as significant factors in educational policy and practice. It then follows naturally that with a view like the one suggested, decisions of such members are likely to be informed by these factors. With such convergence of vision, it becomes easier for such members to work with a set of data that they considered questionable. This suggests, therefore, that the twin themes of the economy and the labour market had substantial influence on the shape and direction of the adult literacy policy that was developed by the committee and that the influential value position was inevitably instrumental and human capital orientated.

Some responses from members of the committee interviewed lend some credence to this thesis. One respondent's contribution illustrates the attitude of members towards the issue of validity or otherwise of the tool. When asked about his opinion with respect to the nature and validity of the data, this respondent said: 'In a sense, I didn't mind whether it was accurate or inaccurate, but the fact that it got them thinking about it is important.' This response suggests that some members might have gone along on the basis of a vision that might not necessarily have converged with that of the government. Nevertheless, it demonstrated the fact that some members knew that the picture painted by the data could have been deceptive. However, there were responses from other members which corroborated the convergence of vision and the predetermined agenda arguments. One such respondent captures this line of argument in his response:

> Personally, I've always been in favour of making up statistics... And what we wanted to do, and my prime goal, was to make the case for the government to put in money. That was it, so actually I couldn't care a toss about.

There is, however, another thread of argument emerging from the responses of other members interviewed. Although many members recognised the limitations of the data, they were happy to overlook this because the alarming claim of the data was likely to strengthen the case for the government to allocate more funds to the endeavour. There is a possibility emerging from this that some members could have been pliant even though their vision did not converge with those of the government. For such members, it is possible that a vision of empowerment and

DOI: 10.1057/9781137535115.0004

widening participation was primary in their consideration. One such respondent declared:

> That the figures really, you know, if – and in fact if they want to exaggerate the figures, at that point in the game, good, let's go for it. Because what we want to do is to get everybody scared to death really, so that they'll chuck in the money.

Thus, there is some evidence that with differing visions and goals, many members of the committee were compliant for economic considerations, ranging between the need to justify economic outlay and the desire to have as much funding as possible for the adult literacy project. This, in our view, is another pointer to the dominant influence of the instrumental/human capital value position that drove the adult literacy policy agenda at this stage.

Also significant is the acknowledgement of the fact that many members of the committee accepted the data from a tool they were suspicious of because it provided some form of framework for international comparison. Linked closely to the issue of comparative international level of literacy gap is the notion of competition in the European labour market. It is clear that at this stage, there was apprehension about the potential disadvantage that workers in Britain might have when compared to their European counterparts. This apprehension, it could be argued, was fuelled by the emerging competitive nature of the labour market, which now demands highly skilled manpower. Pring (2005, 2006) argues that the incumbent labour government had a perception that 'the country needed...highly skilled workforce in a very competitive world'. This perception led to the emergence of 'a moral drive for greater social inclusion and an economic drive for greater prosperity' (2006, p.428).

The literacy problem as portrayed by the OECD research tool, therefore, provided an opportunity to legitimise, especially, the economic drive. It is, therefore, understandable that many members of the committee who shared the vision of the government and who were possibly included in the committee for this reason were very willing to embrace the one-sided statistics provided by the OECD survey.

Following from the ongoing, therefore, we suggest that the subscription of the members of the committee to the OECD data, which many perceived as flawed, was driven by both economic and labour market considerations. Some respondents acknowledged this element of wanting to be competitive with our European rivals both economically and in the

DOI: 10.1057/9781137535115.0004

labour market. One such acknowledgement puts the Moser Committee's emergence in perspective while also offering reasons for accepting whole-heartedly data that many perceived as flawed. The following sums up the perception of this respondent in respect of this issue:

> Well, I think there were political priorities. I mean all this Moser Committee is very much product of the New Labour government in 1997 ... desperate not to throw overboard its predecessor, the Thatcher government's on Britain being the weak man of Europe, ... hopeless economically ... and so they were absolutely obsessed with this idea of trying to catch up with continental levels and skills and were absolutely appalled by this 22 per cent who were supposed to have the reading age of ten-year-olds.

Another respondent highlighted the role of economic and employment factors in the members' view of the tool that provided the baseline data. When asked about the alignment of the OECD tool to a paradigm of literacy that takes a one-sided view of literacy, the respondent defined what in his view was most important to most members of the committee in the following quote:

> I mean the real thrust of it was more around the employability and the social aspects of literacy. The economic consequences of one in eight people not being of a level of the expected average of a primary person to be ... it was more socio-economic.

A deduction that could be made from this is that because of its emphasis on the economic consequences of literacy problems, the OECD data was accepted as the economic rationale, overshadowed all other argument, but more importantly, converged with the dominant instrumental/ human capital value position. In an indirect way, therefore, the themes of the economy and the labour market, but this time in the context of international competitiveness, were very significant in the direction and shape of adult literacy policy.

Possible influence of socio-economic factors

This interview sought to identify the social factors that members of the committee considered influential in the decisions they arrived at. The rationale behind this line of questioning was to establish if members had a perception that their work was targeted at addressing particular issues, and in effect confirm the extent to which these issues might have affected the decisions they took in terms of shaping the adult literacy policy. Although the term social was used generically here, in the course of the interview, respondents were encouraged to look at the wider ramifications of the term and to extend it to cover social issues like structure, the economy, employment and indeed the entire social components of the welfare state.

It is perhaps significant that there were conflicting views on the significance of the social factors in the deliberations of the committee. While some members simply claimed that such factors played no role and that 'it was not in our remit', others confirmed that some of the decisions made were informed by their perception of the prevalent social situation. This divergence in perception might itself be significant in terms of power relations within the committee. In our view, it raises the possibility that some members were simply attendees or merely named members who contributed very little to the whole process. Presented here are the significant social factors identified by the members interviewed.

1   Many members interviewed believe that the vision of societal prosperity that could be associated with improved basic skills was influential in decision making. They linked this perception to the work done by the National Skills Taskforce which served as a beacon for some members of the committee.
2   Some members identified the comparative location of Britain in the European context using the index of economic growth and employment.
3   Some members identified the social state of employability and 'worklessness' as highly significant in shaping the direction of policy.
4   Another view identified what was considered to be the huge outlay of government in the attempt to bear the burden of unemployment.
5   Some members thought that the influence of the private sector, particularly the views of the Institute of Directors, was highly significant.
6   Another view from the respondents was that there were social issues that had been identified before the committee was convened and that the role of the committee was to find solutions to these issues. As such, finding solutions to these issues was considered extremely significant in shaping the direction of policy.

DOI: 10.1057/9781137535115.0004

7   Some respondents, while agreeing with these, view identified skills, economy and empowerments as social issues that informed the direction of policy.

8   Some members identified the collapse of the manufacturing industry, and the subsequent rise of the service industry was very significant.

There is no doubt that most members of the committee were of the view that decisions made in the committee were informed in varying degrees by their perception of a range of social factors. In the first place, responses from many members indicated that the starting point was the perception or the view held by many members of the state of the economy and the labour market. A comment from one of the members interviewed corroborates this perception. In the opinion of this member, there is no doubt that the issues of the economy and the labour market were foremost in the minds of some members of the committee and played a very significant role in the shaping of the policy:

> [T]here was no doubt that one of the main lines that the committee wanted to think about was the impact that improved basic skills might have economi-cally and, essentially that means in terms of getting people-either getting them, so they are participating in the world of work at all, you know, they are currently coming to the point where because they are literate or more numerate then they are better able to, you know, they are a bit more flexible in terms of work.

A similar argument is further encapsulated in the following comment by another respondent:

> And so that the economic argument was really important, it was part of the template of a lot of people in that committee.... there was [sic] people in that group who started at that point....* for example certainly saw a basis for part of the literacy thing at work. And that led to arguments in the committee about whether in effect it is all about unemployment and that we should have a compulsory literacy and numeracy test. It wasn't a wish to be nasty to unemployed people, but actually the thought that this was going to be one of the things that would be particularly important in getting them out and out of unemployment. And I think there is something in that argument.

From these responses, it would seem that many members of the commit-tee were influenced by their perception of the existing social situation in terms of unemployment and the economy. This line of thought is further given credibility in the context of the chronicled deplored state

DOI: 10.1057/9781137535115.0004

of unemployment at the onset of the New Labour government in 1997. It is natural to expect that this perceived state of 'unacceptable level of unemployment', which many influential employers forum blamed on poor literacy and numeracy, will form part of the socio-cognitive realities of some members. This in turn, it is to be expected, will inform the established value position that these members bring into the policy-making process.

But it is also important to consider the role of the government in bringing these social factors into the consciousness of some of the members. There are two issues to explore in this respect. Were the members who recognised the importance of the economic and unemployment factors so influenced by the pre-determined agenda of the government or were they in the first place made members of the committee because of their known inclinations in terms of their responses to these social factors? While there was no clear evidence from respondents on this issue, it is safe to simply note that these factors played a significant role in the way some members saw the responsibility they had within the committee.

One respondent painted a much more distinct picture of how the issues of employment and the economy were pushed into the policy-shaping agenda by employers within the society. This respondent suggested that the view held by employers on why there was so much unemployment was to do with skill shortage on the part of the people. This view is captured in the following claim:

> I mean the view was that employers felt that people, the workers, were just hopeless, you know inadequate…it was put to us that employers were just, couldn't deal with how bad, you know, the workforce was, and it was considered the reason they weren't employing people was because they lacked these skills.

The revelation from this respondent suggests that the views of employers on the social state of employment/unemployment as presented to the members of the committee must have played a significant role and possibly coloured the judgements of some members. In effect, the twin themes of unemployment and the economy have again proved highly influential in the shaping and direction of adult literacy policy in the context of the Moser Committee. More importantly, these themes extended an instrumental and human capital value position to policymaking in the field.

Another significant issue is the revelation that the perception of Britain's position in the context of international comparison played a

DOI: 10.1057/9781137535115.0004

significant role in the shaping of policy. While it is true that there is an international dimension to this argument, it is important to note that the features subjected to international comparison were local to the different countries being compared. In the context of Britain, the main features that were subjected to international comparison were the elements of employability and self-sustenance. While the former aligns naturally to the economy and wealth creation variables, the latter would appear to subscribe to the empowerment and inclusiveness argument. Shortly before and during the deliberations of the Moser Committee, there were debates about the comparative status of the workforce in Britain relative to our European counterparts and also about the comparative number of people on the unemployment/income benefit. Conveniently spliced to these were issues around the number of people who were unable to carry out day-to-day chores for which literacy is required. This again was usually located in the context of the overall picture of what is in place across the industrialised world. The perception of the relative state of the economy and unemployment pattern could, therefore, be seen as very significant for many members. One respondent noted:

> Britain being the weak man of Europe means em... so that was one priority, the economic. I mean yes that was really the driver from the political priorities of the government.

But the same respondent acknowledged, the humanist response to some of the social issues that could have informed the decisions taken in the process of policy formation. According to this respondent,

> the other, of course, was this government, its more humane social face was about social exclusion. It set up the social exclusion unit, it developed a whole string of policies around the idea which comes originally from France of everybody should be able to participate in the society.

The response from this member underscores the significance of the international comparison of local social factors, not only from the viewpoint of the economy, but also from the more humane angle of social inclusiveness. But putting the significance of the comparative dimension of social setting in a clearer context is the comment of another respondent who argues that prior to the convening of the Moser Committee, issues such as the collapse of the manufacturing and mining industries had already become matters of concern. However,

DOI: 10.1057/9781137535115.0004

what hadn't been predicted was that we would become dependent on Eastern Europe and a new range of immigrants would come and so on. I mean that wasn't on the horizon at all. And that might have changed the conversation somewhat.

This comment again provides a glimpse into one of the factors that must have played a significant role in the decision making of some members of the committee. While Britain was seen as inviting foreigners to take up jobs that British people could not take on because of their lack of literacy and numeracy, it would seem that this was not the case with countries of comparable status like Germany and France. Hence, it was logical that this social state of event would again inform the socio-cognitive themes some members brought to the policymaking process. This undoubtedly would have impacted on the positions they took during the deliberations of the committee.

Another significant social factor was the gradual demise of the manufacturing and mining industry and the attendant emergence of the service industry. There are two key issues about this. First is the fact that with the decline of the manufacturing and mining industries, many workers were laid off and had become part of the unemployment statistics at the time the committee began its work. Closely related to this is the fact that many of these unemployed people were unable to take up the newly created jobs because of their limitations in the field of literacy and other basic skills. This social situation thus leaves room for the employers' forum to exert influence in terms of the direction of the adult literacy policy. This view resonates in the comment of one member, who was not in doubt that some of the policy decisions made by the committee

> were driven to some extent by the views of the private sector expressing the CPI, Institute of Directors, about the shocking and appalling nature of standards in this country around literacy and numeracy and the blame sort, sort of blame culture developed around the schools.

All of this becomes more meaningful against the backdrop of the report of an earlier commission, the Hamlin Commission, which incidentally was chaired by the chairman of the Moser Committee. The focus of this report was on what some have described as the perception of the inadequacy of education, education as a failing system and the fact that going through education is more significant because there are fewer jobs on offer and only those with the proper educational background could secure those jobs. Hamlin's Report, conceivably, could be seen as the

DOI: 10.1057/9781137535115.0004

backdrop against which the perception of the need for any educational policy to consider the issue of employment and job skills becomes more significant. This, then, was one of the more important social impetuses that shaped the form and direction of adult literacy policy through the Moser Committee, a perception that adult literacy must be delivered in a way that should help address the problems of unemployment, skill shortages in the labour market, as well as issues of social deprivation. From the responses of many members of the committee interviewed, it was evident that all of these must have registered in the subconscious of many members of the committee. As one respondent puts it, 'people on the committee were well aware of the social causes and consequences of um... er... the social and economic consequences of people having er... poor literacy and numeracy skills'.

The crucial questions here are twofold. First, through what medium were these issues introduced into the consciousness of these members? There are two possibilities. On the one hand, it might be through the government and its agents who in the first place brought these members into the committee. If that was the case, we are again re-visiting the issue of a pre-determined agenda. On the other hand, these notions could have been developed by individuals through their perception of the socio-cognitive reality of events happening within the society. If this was the case, it raises the issue of possible convergence of views and vision with those of the government which, as we have argued earlier, might be responsible in the first place for the composition of the committee.

The second question revolves around the appreciation of the causes of the social problems that were endemic within the society at the time. Within the committee, it appeared that the consensus was that the problems were caused by the people and the educational system. This raises the notion of a value position that has had currency in the past decade and that sees education as cause and remedy for social ills. This, of course, ties in with the argument we have pushed throughout this book that there is a convergence between the direction of travel of adult literacy policy and the value positions of instrumentalism and human capital.

The essence of the views held by committee members can be seen from two angles. First, there is the age-long justification of outlay in terms of economic return, and second, there is the issue around the goals of education and what ought to be included in a curriculum. Either way, the related value positions of instrumentalism and human capital

DOI: 10.1057/9781137535115.0004

appear to be the most suited to the rationales offered by the members of the committee for the policy positions they took. For us, therefore, these two value positions were in the ascendancy in terms of determining the direction and nature of adult literacy policy.

Possible significant political factors

This interview sought to establish the interviewed members' view on the extent to which prevalent political factors influenced the direction and shape of the adult literacy policy developed by the Moser Committee. The rationale for this line of enquiry was the need to verify claims that the policy that emerged from the work of the committee was the result of a dominant political ideology and as a result a by-product of a dominant value position. Answers in response to this line of enquiry would enable us to draw a link between political viewpoints and educational policy development and would serve as the basis for definitive statements on the alignment of political ideology to literacy policy. The findings in this respect are summarised as follows.

1   To some respondents, the political is inexorably linked to the social and economic.
2   Most respondents acknowledged that whatever political factor was seen as influential originated from an economic ideology.
3   Some respondents who recognised the influence of political factors also acknowledged the impact of what they call New Labour Ideology.
4   A few respondents felt that there were competing political ideologies which include a political philosophy of 'empowerment/ do-gooder and the economy'.

There is a strong indication from many respondents who felt that the major political factor that was influential in the evolution of policy through the Moser Committee was the overarching New Labour Ideology. Many acknowledged the convergence between the direction of policy, as it was informed by the composition, mandate and other factors already discussed, and the visions of the then newly elected Labour government. But what is the political ideology of the New Labour with respect to education? A significant number of commentators on the New Labour policy consider its policy on education as one that is centred on

DOI: 10.1057/9781137535115.0004

the development of skills in the context of economic development. For example, Pring (2005, p.418) sums up the New Labour policy on education in the term 'Skills Revolution'. Encapsulating the importance of the twin factors of skills and the economy in the development of New Labour policy in the field of education is the 2003 white paper, '21st Century Skills: Realising Our Potential'. For many commentators, the aim of the policy position presented in this document was 'to provide a framework in which Britain might prosper economically in highly competitive world' (p.418). It becomes apparent, therefore, that the issue of economic prosperity is very important in the equation that generates the New Labour policy on education. But the notion of economic prosperity is not a unilateral factor. Rather, it is seen in the context of its relationship with a related concept of training and skills as facilitators of economic prosperity, with employers and government agencies as key participants in this revolution. Pring (2005) sums up this position noting,

> The essential ingredient is a skills revolution – ensuring that many more people acquire relevant skills. Education providers play a crucial role in this, but that role must be seen within the wider context of a partnership with employers, the Regional Development Agencies, the (occupational) Sector Skills Councils and the local learning and Skills Councils. (p.418)

What this configuration drives home is the importance that the government places on economic prosperity, but more importantly, the role that training, skills and the evolution of vocations must play in achieving the goal of economic prosperity. In a sense, therefore, the policy of the government was informed by a value position which holds that education must be seen in the first place, as the cause of socio-economic dysfunction and, by implication, as the remedy for these dysfunctions. This position tallies with arguments of scholars who have chronicled the government's shift from a policy position that now sees education as both cause and remedy, rather than as a symptom of social dysfunctions (see, e.g., Ade-Ojo, 2011; Allen and Ainley, 2007; Pring, 2005; Ball, 2004).

Other factors

This section focuses on responses from members to the invitation to identify other factors that have not been covered previously. The rationale for this was to provide opportunities to the members of the

DOI: 10.1057/9781137535115.0004

committee to offer their opinions outside of the semi-structured focus of the interview. This, it was expected, would leave room for independent reflection on events.

A key issue identified in this context centres around what members of the committee referred to as 'the international factor'. Many members identified an element of international influence on the deliberations of the committee. The nature of the mentioned international influence can be subsumed under the notions of existing practice and economic competitiveness. The most cited international influence in the context of existing practice was the influence of America.

There was an indication that while some members of the committee were not particularly enthusiastic about a possible American template, what had happened in America, nevertheless, had some influence. One respondent captured this in the following statement: 'But there was a little bit of a sense that, you know, *** was going to come and tell us how to do it, which some of them didn't care for very much.'

This discussion arose from the fact that an American, who had been involved in a similar project, had been invited to contribute to the deliberations of the committee. This in itself was an irony because there had been occasions where people had actually gone to America to present papers on how America might learn from the British approach to Basic skills development. One respondent's view was that the influence of America as represented by the invited practitioner was not really towards developing policy. Rather, it was to help paint a clearer picture of the urgency of the problem and how this related to the economic well-being of the Western world. In this respondent's words (American representatives),

> what they did do, of course, was, you know, paint a sharper picture in a sense of how important all this was, how urgent it was, but also a sense of a general Western problem.

But the response from another member confirms the view that some members were happy looking at the template from America. This respondent describes the session where an American representative had a presentation as 'probably the best session we had ... he gave us – a presentation to the committee, which was absolutely excellent'.

But the crucial question is what exactly the committee learnt from America. Which aspects of the committee's decisions were influenced by the American worldview? There was very little evidence to help determine the extent of American influence. Indeed most respondents were

DOI: 10.1057/9781137535115.0004

very vague about it in a rather surprising manner, considering that it was a factor that was unanimously identified by virtually all. One respondent, however, gave an indication of what the role of the American experience might have been. In this respondent's view, it was more a question of helping to conceptualise the problems faced by Britain as it was considered similar to those faced by the Americans. In this respondent's view, many members of the committee:

> 'thought we shared the same problem'. In terms of the presentation made by the American representative, the respondent felt that the presenter 'was a very important witness to the committee, and made a lot of very good points and which also showed that you know, the issues that we were confronting here were similar in the states for example'.

Though it is difficult to confirm the nature of the American influence in the committee's decision, what we could, however, confirm is the fact that members of the committee were aware of the situation in America, and also of the measures that had been taken to combat what some might consider similar problems. If this had any influence on the decisions of the committee, it was certainly not in any institutionalised form. What we might be able to infer is that the knowledge that was made available to members could possibly have unconsciously influenced some members. How this happened is in our view an entirely cognitive process and, therefore, very difficult to tease out.

Despite this vagueness, subsequent work in the area of adult literacy policy in America confirms the instrumental/human capital driver behind policy (see, e.g., Beauregard, 2009). Given the similarities between America and the United Kingdom in the context of the economy and employment at this time, there is a case to be made for expecting a similar value position to be influential across the two closely related countries. Whether there is a justification to this claim we shall attempt to explore in the brief section on the international dimensions of adult literacy policy later in this chapter.

In contrast to the vagueness of responses in respect of how practice in America might have influenced decisions on the committee, the notion of international influence on the basis of competitiveness was clearly acknowledged by many members interviewed. In this respect, the issue of the economy again rears its head. From the responses of members to the question of international influence, it was obvious that the nature of the influence was informed by comparisons with other countries on the

DOI: 10.1057/9781137535115.0004

economic front. This, of course, was informed by a perception that there is a strong link between literacy and employability of individuals and the overall economic well-being of the society. Reinforcing this relationship is the contribution from one respondent who said:

> Well certainly as I say, we looked at all the international comparisons, I mean we were sort of shown the league tables of where we were as the UK in relation to Sweden, Finland, Czech Republic, you know, USA, Australia and all the rest of it, and I think we were given the impression that you know, we have got to do better than this, that was one of the drivers, ... you know the international comparisons and economic competitors put in front of us. And you know if you don't sort this out, you know we will get further behind, I wouldn't say that was done in a threatening way but there was a little bit of that.

Another respondent highlighted the theme of international influence through a drive for economic competitiveness in this response:

> I think the whole um ... skills agenda in the early years of the Labour admin-istration was very much led by a fear that Britain was losing its place in the world.. and a concern that Britain may lose its competitive edge in key industries and services was due to a skills gap and I think it is fair to say that was ... that was broadly accepted by the majority of people on the committee.

For others, the only aspect of the committee's deliberations that was influenced by globalisation and international influence was firmly related to the economy. The following statement sums up this view:

> and Britain feels by de-regulating more than other European countries that it's done pretty well on this, but you can see the Skills for Life as very much part of that, yeah to win global competitions or assist the British labour market to keep up.

From the ongoing, it is clear that there was some sort of international influence, but not from the viewpoint of practice. Evidence provided by respondents suggests that the international factor was strongly aligned to the twin factors of the economy and the labour market. It was evident that many members of the committee felt that some of their decisions were informed by an apprehension of how Britain compared interna-tionally economically and in the labour market. What was, however, not made transparent was the source of introducing this apprehension. Did members isolate this of their own volition, or were they influenced by the myriad of international data presented to them? If the latter were the

DOI: 10.1057/9781137535115.0004

case, this might in a way provide evidence to support the argument that there was an element of pre-determination and that the committee was effectively handed a fait accompli. If the former were the case, however, we could assume that it was a natural process for members to bring to committee deliberations the socio-cognitive reality of their existence in the international sphere. Whichever was the case, responses from members make it clear that some decisions were probably made in the context of the international economic and labour market discourse, and, therefore, driven by an instrumental value position.

Other relevant policies pre and post-Moser

Other educational policies generated by the government before and since the Moser Committee's SfL policy appear to corroborate the argument that the overarching political/educational policy of the government is firmly driven by the instrumental assumption that education should be seen as a tool for wealth creation, a position which is usually reinforced through vocationalisation, skills upgradation and employment argument. A number of the policies that were generated before and since Moser all bear the hallmark of instrumental economic determinism.

One of the policies that reflects this perception is the Kennedy Report of 1997. While appraising the impact of the policy, Silver (2007) puts this into perspective in her reflection on ten years of the policy. She acknowledges that there were three value strands, namely, greater participation, learning for social improvement and the economic potential of skills development, which underpinned the Kennedy Report. In her view, however, only the economic value has truly flourished as '[l]ifelong learning and its fundamental value to the learner, their family and their community has dwindled' (p.1). Presumably, this has happened because of the pre-eminence of the influence of the economic value strand. It is evident from this that the political ideology that dictates the government's educational policy is inexorably linked to the arguments of economic relevance.

Another policy that corroborates the highlighted political leaning of the government is the citizenship education policy based on the final version of the Crick Report (1998). Ostensibly, the policy was not geared towards education per se. Nevertheless, it serves as an illustration of

DOI: 10.1057/9781137535115.0004

how hidden values are embedded in educational policy, in particular, a value that is informed by instrumental economic argument. On the face of it, the Crick Report, and by implication, the government's policy, demand that citizenship 'be recognised as a vital and distinct statutory part of the curriculum, an entitlement for pupils in its own right' (QCA, 1998, p.31). However, many commentators have argued that there is another side to the policy, a side, which in our view, is instrumental and firmly linked to the notion of providing supplements for a failing welfare state. Presenting a similar argument, Larkin (2001) argues that:

> at least on one level, the citizenship directive is an attempt to curb perceived, endemic, antisocial, and disengaged behaviour of the young people of this country rather than merely educating them in the workings of the body polity. (p.1)

This view can be extended to cover the arguments about the economic benefits of such rehabilitation of young people to the state. But making a clearer statement on the relevance of the economy and skills development is McLaughlin (2000, p.549) who argues that the component of political literacy in the citizenship directive should be 'seen as involving not only the acquisition of political knowledge ... but pupils' learning about and how to make themselves effective in public life through knowledge skills and values'. This argument again locates the Crick Report and the attendant government directive in the context of instrumentalism, which in this case is informed by economic outcomes.

Pykett (2007) provides a more functional analysis of the Crick Report by locating it within the discourse context of a range of other policies, which in her view contributes to the interpretation of the true intentions of the directive. Within the context of previous policies such as the 1997 Excellence in Schools policy, Pykett identifies the strand of what she calls 'education as a social panacea' (p.304). In a similar vein, and along with Ball (2003), she argues that the real intention of another policy, Schools Achieving Success, is embedded in such terms as 'tightening control', 'accountability', 'intervention', 'greater choice for consumers' and 'better incentives for performance'. She then concludes that

> Taken together with the Crick Report, these initiatives form the backdrop to an agenda which is dominated by standards, flexibility and the behaviour of the whole child as citizen in order to maintain the 'economic health and social cohesion of the country'. (Ball, 2003, p.219; DFES, 2001, p.5)

DOI: 10.1057/9781137535115.0004

What the above confirms is the fact that there are two levels to the analysis of most policies on education. While at the surface is a nodal discourse, which might proclaim one intention, there is always a hidden imperative which ultimately signifies a different intention. In this case, evidence from many of the policies examined suggests that the economy, employment and skill development are usually the hidden values behind most policy initiatives in education.

More recently, the Foster Report and the Leitch Review of Skills both display similar patterns to the one identified. The Foster Report and the government white paper generated in response to it, though ostensibly looking at the position of FE colleges within the framework of education, again demonstrate the commitment to the notions of employability and economic competitiveness in the global economy. This policy is particularly significant in the context of adult literacy policy because it focuses on further education, which is essentially the dominant provider of adult literacy. In the vision of his proposed educational reform, Foster (2005) emphasises the following:

> The need to maximise and fulfil the potential of all our people – young people and adults – to contribute knowledge and skills of world class quality in competitive proportion to the size of our population. Future economic prosperity and good public services depend on this. (p.9)

The report goes further to highlight among others what needs to be done in order to achieve this vision:

> To achieve its place in the world economy, the UK needs an education and skills system that creates a pool of skilled and mobile employees, and re-trains workers to keep pace with changing technology. (p.1)

The line of reasoning presented in the Foster Report is followed through in the government policy paper, 'Further Education: Raising Skills, Improving Life Chances' (2006). In its executive summary, the paper identifies the following among others as purpose of the policy:

> our future as a prosperous nation depends on our education and training system. We rely on the system to prepare and develop young people fully for life, and to develop in both young people and adults the skills that are necessary for the productive and competitive economy. (p.3)

An additional purpose which is relevant here is for the FE system to 'be a powerhouse for delivering skills at all levels that are needed to sustain an advanced, competitive economy' (p.3).

DOI: 10.1057/9781137535115.0004

What the cited visions and purposes of both the policy document and its prelude, the Foster Report, confirm is that there has been a change in the discourse of education as an intrinsic pursuit to an instrumental pursuit. Within the context of the ongoing discourse, it is perhaps safe to see the economy, the labour market, skills development and international competitiveness as indices of the instrumental focus of educational policies.

The Leitch Report in its review of skills again tells a similar story. A number of declarations in the foreword to the final report encapsulate the notion of skills development as an all-consuming factor in education. Among the striking comments made in the foreword to the final report (2006) are the following: 'our natural resource is our people – and their potential is both untapped and vast. Skills will unlock that potential' (p.1); 'skills matter fundamentally for the economic and social health of the UK' (p.1); 'Our nation's skills are not world class and we run the risk that this will undermine the UK's long-term prosperity' (p.1); 'Our skill base compares poorly, and critically, all of our comparators are improving' (p.2). The sentiments embodied by these citations is manifested in some of the final recommendations, including 'Increase adult skills across all levels'; 'Strengthen employer voice'; 'Increase employer engagement and investment in skills' (p.4). All of the citations again highlight the devotion to skill development for economic sustenance and prosperity in the guise of educational policy. There is no doubt that from the perception of Leitch and those who believe in his vision, economically viable skills should be the foundation of any curriculum, particularly those developed for young people and adults. The Leitch Report set ambitious goals that impact SfL. Some of the objectives include:

- 95 per cent of adults to achieve the basic skills of functional literacy and numeracy, an increase from levels of 85 per cent literacy and 79 per cent numeracy in 2005
- exceeding 90 per cent of adults qualified to at least Level 2, an increase from 69 per cent in 2005
- a commitment to go further and achieve 95 per cent as soon as possible; shifting the balance of intermediate skills from Level 2 to Level 3. Improving the esteem, quantity and quality of intermediate skills. This means 1.9 million additional Level 3 attainments over the period and boosting the number of Apprentices to 500,000 a year; exceeding 40 per cent of adults qualified to Level 4 and above, up from 29 per cent in 2005, with a commitment to continue progression. (Leitch, 2006, p.3)

DOI: 10.1057/9781137535115.0004

Although the then incumbent Labour government did not publicly own up to the fact that its political ideology is driven by a consummate drive for skills development for economic purposes, the slant of its policies over the years in the field of education suggests that this might be the case. For a committee like Moser's, therefore, working under the influence of a government political and educational policy focus that is targeted on skills development for economic prosperity through education and training, it is to be expected that these factors will be very significant in the deliberations of the Moser Committee. In a way, this again highlights the blurred boundaries between the socio-economic and socio-political factors in the development of policy. As this case seems to demonstrate, one is likely to generate the other.

As it were, literacy is now subsumed under another label of functional skills, which is perhaps part of the government's response to the Leitch Report. Essentially, the concept of functional skills again emphasises the commitment of the government towards a vision of education for employment purposes. This inclination is captured in the QCA's description of 'how functional skills will contribute to the adult skills agenda'. It makes no secret of the fact that the ultimate goal is to tackle the skills gap in England as indicated in the following quote:

> The development of 'functional' skills for adults is crucial to tackling the skills gap in England. Helping adults improve their levels of 'functional' English, mathematics and ICT will support employers' needs to have a workforce that is enterprising, productive and equipped to compete in business. These skills will also assist adults to interact confidently within their communities. (QCA, 2006)

We can, therefore, deduce that the government, as it was at the inception of the Moser Committee, remains consumed by the perception of education in general, and literacy in particular, as one of the solutions to a range of social ills, conspicuous among which is a perceived skills gap which has continued to fail both the citizens and the employers.

Summary

Drawing from the series of responses from respondents, this section established the fact that there were a range of factors that significantly shaped many of the decisions taken in the committee, which effectively

DOI: 10.1057/9781137535115.0004

resulted in the adult literacy policy embedded in the SfL agenda. While some of these factors impacted directly on the members of the committee and their agenda, others impacted in a rather indirect way. What the findings discussed have enabled us to do is to corroborate the argument that the dominant value positions that informed policy development at the time of the Moser Committee had evolved in the same manner that the policy itself had evolved. Indeed, it has helped to confirm the argument that policy evolution was in tandem with the evolution of influential factors. Specifically, adult literacy policy has evolved from the influence of factors related to the needs of learners in the 1970s to the influence of factors more recognised from the viewpoint of the funders, the government.

Evidence collated from members of the committee suggests that the most important factors were the economy, labour market and international competitiveness. These themes were continuously found to be influential, either through a pre-determined government agenda or through the socio-cognitive realities of members of the committee, who consistently pushed them into positions of prominence in the committee's deliberations. This change in policy influence and direction, it is expected, will have influence on practice. How this has manifested in the context of adult literacy provision in the years since the Moser Committee is not a specific concern of ours here.

It is, however, important that we note here that the policy generated by the Moser Committee was not really a product of total consensus. Rather, a lot of compromises were arrived at, and some members simply acceded because they felt that there was some good in it for the field of adult literacy and numeracy. In the words of one respondent,

> The reason the consensus didn't lead to, didn't break down, I mean we, it was desperate to keep the committee together on final recommendations and that was because pleas came through from the adult education area which said for God's sake this is the first time this area has ever had any real attention and the possibility of money, large money, because it's always been the poor relation, ... it doesn't matter what the committee comes up with because it is strong and powerful it'll attract funding and that persuaded one or two people like myself to sort of think.

Thus, we see that the policy generated by the committee was not the product of a unified vision, but a child of compromise of views, visions and ideologies.

DOI: 10.1057/9781137535115.0004

Conclusion

Increased attention has been paid to literacy in the past two decades, predominantly among countries participating in the Organisation for Economic Co-operation and Development (OECD) (Carey, 2000; Grek, 2010; Sellar and Lingard, 2013; Hamilton, 2014). The OECD's 2013 report makes clear that the instrument for measuring literacy levels across countries is the specifically designed OECD programme for the international assessment of adult competencies (PIAAC). Policy discourses, which arise from the placing of literacy where it is valued almost exclusively in economistic terms, position literacy as the foundation for employability and integral to the economic competitiveness of industry and nations (Sellar and Lingard, 2013). Literacy being increasingly conceived primarily in terms of human capital expressed, for example, as 'functional' skills that enable individuals, as well as enterprises and nations, to become more productive and competitive in the labour market based on the premise of a 'knowledge economy'. Within this premise one of the most significant duties given to education is to provide a flexible, adaptable and skilled workforce to make countries competitive in the globalised economy. It focuses on education for work purposes and education as a commodity and pays no regard to issues of economic, political and social equality. For example, learners from socio-economically deprived areas may not have the same access to opportunities as those who live in more affluent areas who would be more able to attend high-achieving state schools or receive a private education (Duckworth, 2013, p.14). Thus, school success may be seen as linked by 'the amount and type of cultural capital inherited from the family milieu rather than by measures of individual talent or achievement' (Reay et al., 2005, p.19). For the children who face such structural inequalities, the choices they have on leaving school or college can be limited and can impact on their life chances, opportunities for future education or training and future employment.

DOI: 10.1057/9781137535115.0004

4
Exploring an Alternative: A Transformative Curriculum Driven by Social Capital

Abstract: *This chapter explores the potential alternatives to the dominant philosophy, policy and practice. Informed by sociological and critical educational frames that recognise the political, social and economic factors that conspire to marginalise learners, it offers a transformative approach to adult literacy whilst locating the model in an underpinning philosophy. Rich empirical data from practice is probed to offer a justification to the recognition accorded the model. The analysis argues that a different value position to the dominant curriculum could yield a different approach to practice. This is illustrated with transformative and emancipatory literacy, which derives its values from a libertarian, equality and justice base (as against an instrumentalist base). We expose how changes to policy and practice would inform and shape the literacy curriculum and indeed pedagogy, a central driver, we also suggest, being adult education/literacy dis-entangling itself from neo-liberal fusion and creating critical space for contextualised and emancipatory learning.*

Keywords: emancipatory learning; empirical research; literacy practice; sociology of education; transformative literacy

Ade-Ojo, Gordon and Vicky Duckworth. *Adult Literacy Policy and Practice: From Intrinsic Values to Instrumentalism.* Basingstoke: Palgrave Macmillan, 2015. DOI: 10.1057/9781137535115.0005.

Introduction

This chapter will explore potential alternatives to the dominant philosophy, policy and practice. In particular, it will offer a transformative model of adult literacy, locate the model in an underpinning philosophy and demonstrate how such a stance could inform practice. It will draw on empirical data from practice in order to justify the recognition accorded the model. The analysis will argue that a different value position to the dominant one could yield a different curriculum as well as a different approach to practice. This will be illustrated with transformative literacy, which derives its values from a libertarian, equality and justice base (as against an instrumentalist base). It will highlight what alternatives we might have in terms of policy and practice and how differently could the literacy curriculum and indeed pedagogy be constructed. Before engaging with this alternative, it is important to ask: why do we need to consider a different value position and, therefore, a different approach to literacy policy and practice? For us, the answer is simple and straightforward: the dominant value position and the attendant approach to practice have failed many marginalised people. It becomes essential for practitioners, therefore, to continue to search for alternatives.

There are a number of recent Basic Skills learner studies that have come from the National Research and Development Centre (NRDC) (for example Bynner and Parsons, 1997, 2003, 2005; Bynner et al., 2001; Barton et al., 2006; the Basic Skills Agency (BSA) Parsons and Bynner, 1998, 2002, 2005; Parsons, 2002; Bynner and Steedman, 1995; and the Scottish Executive, 2001). The 1958 and 1970 British birth cohort studies, known respectively as the National Child Development Study (NCDS) and the 1970 Cohort Study (BCS70), contain key information about the role of literacy and numeracy in adult lives. Members of this cohort have been surveyed in 1975, 1980, 1986, 1991, 1996 and 2000. Some 11,000 of the original cohort are still involved. Bynner and Parsons make use of the data, including reanalysing it with regard to these individuals and tests of their levels of literacy and numeracy, to show how these affect their life course and life chances.

By tracing and exploring the participant's life back to birth, they are able to uncover their circumstances, history and experiences and uncover the contributing factors behind poor skills in adulthood and their consequences for life chances and adults functioning in society. Together with the exploration of literacy and numeracy, these studies

DOI: 10.1057/9781137535115.0005

unpick a wide range of social and economic issues, and can help to make sense of social and economic change and trends. When exploring adult literacy and numeracy, the studies illuminate how these issues relate to other factors in people's lives such as health and well-being, work, gender and family structures.

Providing evidence that the current dominant value position has failed many, Parsons and Bynner (2006), when linking basic skills and employment, highlight:

> full-time employment, starting almost as soon as it had begun in their teens. Around four-fifths of women with Level 1 or higher skills were in paid employment from age 23, compared with around two-thirds of women with Entry 2 numeracy and just half of women with Entry 2 literacy. Women with Entry 2 literacy had experienced almost twice as much unemployment as women with Entry 3 skills and nearly four times as much as women with Level 1 or higher skills. Many women with Entry 2 skills had spent at least twice as much time in a full-time home-care role as women with Level 1 or higher skills by age 34. (NRDC, p.21)

They also confirmed that:

> For women, poor educational achievement underpins poor employment prospects, especially in the non-manual office jobs that young women tend to favour. In contrast to men in this situation, the outcome for low-skilled women is frequently early partnership and parenthood, offering the alternative career path of mother and carer. Though such young women – particularly following partnership breakdown – may be isolated and stressed through poverty and ill health, they are often more able to cope with the help of other women in comparable situations. (p.29)

Many of the people in the studies (including our own; see Duckworth, 2013, p.14) have been let down by the compulsory and post-compulsory system; in this chapter the heart of our rationale is to seek and explore an alternative paradigm from the neo-liberal models based on individualism and competitiveness.

Transformative learning

Transformative learning reflects a particular philosophy for adult education and a conceptual framework for how adults learn. It fits within a constructivist paradigm where individuals construct knowledge through

DOI: 10.1057/9781137535115.0005

their experiences in the world. Mezirow first applied the label 'transformation' in a 1978 study of US women returning to post-secondary study or the workplace after an extended time out for education. Mezirow's (1991) transformation learning theory has since developed into a theory of adult learning which considers the construction and validation of experience. Mezirow (2000) thus explained transformative learning as a process of effecting change in a frame of reference which is influenced throughout our lives, by the development of a succession of concepts, values, feelings, responses and associations that make up our life experience. Our frames of reference help us to understand our experiences in this world and consist of two dimensions: habits of mind and points of view. By the time a learner reaches adulthood, she or he has constructed a worldview and a set of values/ideologies which shape the way experiences are interpreted.

Mezirow's work has led to a transformative learning movement in adult education. Educational thinkers including Thomas Kuhn, Paulo Freire and Jürgen Habermas all influenced Mezirow's work. Although Mezirow's arguments have been criticised for a focus on the individual learning, an overreliance on rationality and a neglect of social, political and cultural contexts, there is no question that many relevant studies have continued to draw from it. For example, Ade-Ojo (2014) and Duckworth (2013, p.14) have drawn on the general principles of his work with the aim of addressing transformative learning in the context of adult literacy. The latter, using Mezirow's framework, in the study of 16 adult literacy learners returning to further education, showed how Mezirow's framework provided a critical space where the learners and the researcher could reflect and move towards a deepened consciousness in which they recognise that they are products of history. As such, they were able to challenge the conditions of oppression (see Freire, 2004), changing the way they interpret their own experience (McGee, 2002) which led to transformation, specifically in the realm of learning as transformation (see Mezirow, 2000).

The concept of emancipatory learning

We further argue that a desired value position is one that promotes emancipatory learning. Such an outcome, we argue further, will address the needs of students/learners as the ones referred to in the studies by

Parson and Bynner and Duckworth mentioned earlier. Emancipatory learning is based upon the transformation of acquired meaning structures, which are grounded on the assumptions brought to the leaning context. A catalyst for this may be when an adult learner examines her/his own assumptions during instrumental or communicative learning. We firmly suggest that emancipatory education should also teach students how to realise and address their personal and social interests and how to make use of the utensils that society provides, for example, the rights as a mother, father, citizen or worker to defend or advocate them. Emancipatory education can also include the teaching of how grassroots democratic groups are shaped and organised.

Emancipatory leaning, then, occurs when the learners' reality is transformed after new insights are brought about through critical reflection. Giroux (1992) suggests that emancipatory learning informed by critical studies can offer opportunities to consider alternative futures, shape new identities and find social alternatives that may be masked by dominant ideologies, discourses and struggles. This view eliminates the instrumental dimension and promotes the intrinsic dimension of education.

Critical pedagogy

We suggest that in challenging inequalities in learners' lives and communities, adult education should reflect a critical pedagogy, providing a curriculum that is culturally relevant, learner driven and socially empowering (Auerbach, 1989; Freire, 1993; Lankshear and McLaren, 1993; Quigley, 1997; Shor, 1992, Giroux, 1997; Lankshear and McLaren, 1992; Duckworth, 2013, p.14). Critical theorists (Bartolomé, 1996; Freire and Macedo, 1987; Lankshear, 1993; Shor, 1992, p.93; Duckworth and Maxwell, 2015) have criticised many adult education courses for applying a prescriptive pre-set structure and curriculum that seldom take into account the background and needs of the individuals involved. These non-critical courses give importance to skills acquisition, for example, they focus exclusively on delivering knowledge relevant to employability and are instrumental in their approach and implementation. Non-critical courses are criticised for ignoring the political, social and economic factors that have conspired to marginalise people in the first place.

Paulo Freire's (1976) seminal text *The Pedagogy of the Oppressed* addresses who and what education is for and whose group interests are

DOI: 10.1057/9781137535115.0005

promoted. Linking literacy with critical pedagogy, he interrogates the ideologies of classroom practice and the banking theory of knowledge. Within this theory, he argues, traditional pedagogical practice is a means to fill the learners with information/knowledge that serves to maintain the status quo of structural inequalities and unjust hierarchies of power. The learners thus come to be passive receivers of information and accepting of the dominant hegemony[1] which rather than empowering working-class students works to demoralise and label them as unknowing (Freire, 1993, p.64).

In Freire's challenge to the 'banking' system he recommended a critical pedagogy model for teaching adult literacy. Educationalist theorists have developed this approach (see Giroux, 1997; Lankshear and McLaren, 1992; Lankshear, 1993; Shor, 1992, p.93; Duckworth, 2013, p.14). They argue that critical adult literacy programmes should be designed around the backgrounds, needs and interests of students and should encourage a "dialogic" (as defined by Freire, 1993) relationship between teachers and students. More important, courses should establish a democratic setting where students are able to use their developing literacy skills to analyse critically their place in society, understand how certain cultural assumptions and biases have placed them, their families and communities at risk (e.g., illiteracy, poverty, homelessness, etc.) and ultimately learn how to challenge the status quo. Critical adult education courses do not simply teach literacy and other basic skills; rather, they provide thinking tools and show students how they can use those skills to transform their lives and the society in which they live. Traditional curriculum draws from a value position which stands in contradistinction to the value position we advocate.

Practitioner challenges to the prescriptive curriculum

Prescriptive approaches to curriculum designs which do not take into account the history or background and needs of learners have been frequently challenged, at least on the theoretical platform. These non-critical curriculums place emphasis on an instrumental approach ignoring the political, social and economic factors that have conspired to marginalise the learners and the communities they live in. Duckworth (2013) illustrates how the researcher, having been born, brought up and living in the emotional and geographical landscape of her learners,

DOI: 10.1057/9781137535115.0005

was immersed in their communities. This immersion allowed her, as a practitioner, a critical positioning whereby she had insider knowledge of their lives, motivations, pressures, hopes and dreams (see Giroux, 1997; Macedo, 1994; Shor, 1992). This critical model moved to a space whereby the learners became co-producers of knowledge. In doing so, there was a shift away from teacher-directed, top-down, commonly imposed and standardised assessments that prescribe the same for all students, regardless of their ability, values, ethnicity, history, their community requirements or their specific contexts. This echoes the all-pervading instrumentalist curriculum with its concepts of standardised curriculum. So we see an alternative emerging to the instrumental via the egalitarian. An egalitarian approach sees a sharing of power between the teacher and the student in learning, the curriculum, its contents and methods. Freire (2006) proposed to do this via 'culture circles'. A 'culture group' is a discussion group in which educators and learners use codifications to engage in dialectic engagement for consciousness raising, liberation, empowerment and transformation. Education for liberation provides a forum open to the empowerment of learners, teachers, and the community, while also providing opportunities for the development of those skills and competencies without which empowerment would be impossible.

Such emancipatory practices encourage autonomy and critical thinking, opening up spaces where learners and communities can ask questions, analyse and subsequently work through effective and meaningful strategies to enhance their situation. Therefore, rather than being pawns of the system they have the opportunity to be actors of their future and active members of their communities. Our educational philosophy informs our practice, which in turn helps to develop our philosophy. Critical perspectives on learning are clear about their drive and purposes: social transformation through emancipation of individuals and their communities from limited or oppressive beliefs and structures towards a more just, equitable and empowering world. And as such, here we can see a positioning that, unlike learning that simply builds skill or knowledge, transformative learning causes an individual to 'come to a new understanding of something that causes a fundamental reordering of the paradigmatic assumptions she holds and leads her to live in a fundamentally different way.... [T]ransformative learning and education entail a fundamental reordering of social relations and practices' (Brookfield, 2003, p.142). This central shift in one's worldview

DOI: 10.1057/9781137535115.0005

or 'meaning perspective' (Mezirow, 1995) emerges from intense critical reflection that challenges previously held beliefs and assumptions.

Approaches to literacy

In light of the transformative and critical approaches to learning we have discussed, we will now consider how the critical ideologies embedded in them can be applied to literacy. Initially, though, it is helpful to consider how the notion of literacy has been understood within disciplines. Theoretical, pedagogical and research activities concerned with aspects of reading and writing have historically been saturated with paradigms from psychology and have aimed to understand reading, writing, spelling and comprehension as cognitive and behavioural processes in order to improve teaching and learning approaches to mastering written texts. Cognitive/psycholinguistic theories do not probe the means by which power relations shape literacy practices. Whilst, Sociocultural perspectives on literacy, on the other hand, include various theories focused on the many ways in which people use literacy in context, which do include a strong emphasis on power relations. Classic early work in sociocultural literacy studies with an explicit educational focus was influenced by developments in the ethnography of communication and sociolinguistics driven by scholars like Hymes (1980), and by Western acceptances of socio-historical psychology and related work done earlier in the century in the Soviet Union by, for example, Vygotsky (1979). Sociocultural perspectives on literacy are related to sociolinguistic conceptualisations of the ways in which language represents culture (see Gee, 1996), the means in which language use differs depending on contexts (Duckworth, 2013), the link between language use and power (Bourdieu, 1991) and, as stated earlier, the ethnography of communication (Hymes, 1994). In encouraging an ethnography of communication, Hymes explains that:

> facets of the cultural values and beliefs, social institutions and forms, roles and personalities, history and ecology of a community may have to be examined in their bearing on communicative events and patterns. (p.12)

Communicative learning focuses on achieving coherence rather than on driving forward more effective control over the cause–effect relationship to improve performance, as in instrumental learning. An example of

DOI: 10.1057/9781137535115.0005

ethnography of communication can be located in Shirley Brice Heath's major ethnographic study of language patterns and effects within community, home and school settings across distinct social groups in a region of the United States. Heath's work (1982, 1983) shows that children from diverse social groups may learn to decode and encode print in the literal sense (ability to read words from a page and write words on a page) without being able to 'cash in' this learning on equitable terms in respect of 'valorised' school literacies. Heath (1982), for example, shows how working-class children performed comparably with middle-class children in entry-level grades on literacy tasks, but fell progressively behind in subsequent grades. This, she argued, was a function of literacy in subsequent grades drawing on particular 'ways' of talking, believing, valuing, acting and living out that transcend prescriptive and mechanical aspects of encoding and decoding texts, and that are differentially accessible within the social practices of different social groups (see Heath, 1982; Gee, 1991). Duckworth's (2013) research drew on the work of Brice Heath to explore the value of the vernacular literacies learners bring to the classroom. At a personal level, literacy lay in the development of self-identity, in their social, cultural and emotional life, happiness and well-being. For the female and male learners in the study, returning to education was a means for them to develop their literacy skills. Literacy was very much linked with their subjectivity and how they viewed their self-worth in the public and private domains of their lives. When considering the vernacular literacies the learners brought to the classroom, they were united in what Brice Heath (1983) describes as their 'way with words' which did not privilege their literacy practices at school or within the Lifelong Learning Sector (LLS). It was also within the classroom that the learners' reading and writing were detached from "ways of being in the world" (Gee, 1992, 2001). These *ways with words* and indeed *ways of being* influenced and shaped their experience at school, the 'choices' they had or did not have and subsequent trajectories as adults. For example, struggling to read and write at school led to the learners being labelled as thick and experiencing symbolic violence. Stella describes her experience:

> I was quite happy as a child I think until I got to the juniors where spelling and writing everything like, the teachers would look on err and spelling I was never good at, me hand writing was terrible I was left handed and one teacher actually tied my left hand to the chair and tried to make me write with me right hand thinking that he was doing good and but I got that distressed I

DOI: 10.1057/9781137535115.0005

went home and I was heartbroken, my mother came into school and I won't say what happened because my mother was a big lady and she wasn't impressed and he honestly thought he was doing me good by trying to make me write with me right hand. And err I always knew there was something wrong with me because I could never take on board proper what was going on in the class room but I never knew what until I got older I realised that I was dyslexic cos I used to think I was thick and I think as you got further up the years into the seniors if weren't coming on with the rest of the classroom you were sort of shoved to the back of the classroom and oh well she doesn't know what she's doing so we'll leave her there. That's what, that's how I think I was labelled as a child because I wasn't taking on board what was coming across in the class room.

School was clearly a place where fear and intimidation was used to try and control the students to conform, even if that conformity had nothing to do with learning, and more to do with being passive. Rather than being unaware of these labels, in a similar vein to the learners in Skeggs' (1997) study, they were aware that they were being viewed in a negative way. However, whilst Skeggs' learners dis-identified with being working class, to avoid shame, the learners in this study resisted the labels in other ways. For example, they ignored teachers, wagged school and pretended they did not care how they were viewed/treated (even though they did).

On the literacy course one student described how:

As soon as I feel confident enough with my writing I'm doing me Level 2 in Care. The ones who are doing it in the rest home now are treated more professionally somehow. Like they get to help with the medicine round.

The development of literacy skills, confidence and self-esteem was linked to the learners seeing other possible's choices in their lives. For many of the learners the adult literacy classes were their last hope of education. This student's reflections at the beginning of the course are seen in the following interview excerpt:

Response: My aim to get on the Level 2 NVQ in Care

Interviewer: That would be great. Have you ever considered that you could go further than that?

Response: What you mean take the Level 3

Interviewer: Yes

Response: Not really. You've got to be really bright to do that. No I'll just about manage [Level] 2. A few people are on it I know and there's a lot of writing and that.

DOI: 10.1057/9781137535115.0005

There was a transformation in the belief that the student could just about 'learn to read and write properly' to aspiring for and realising her dreams. Working as a part of a collective was a way for the learners to begin to see themselves differently as individuals and question their positioning in unbalanced power relationships that have marginalised them and their practices of literacy, and act to change them. This student progressed to Level 2 and completed Level 3 in Health and Social Care. The cultural capital Stella developed led to resistance and empowerment for her family and self.

Rather than the learners' stories being hidden in shame they took ownership of them. They reclaimed them as stories of success recognising the structural inequalities they have challenged and resisted to become empowered to take agency in their lives. The very words that they had feared and struggled with when they commenced the literacy classes are now tools which they use to re-claim identities that are not stigmatised by struggling with a lack of linguistic capital but are celebrated for using linguistic capital to tell their story, put their voices in the public domain and offer them choices in the avenues they travel in the public and private areas of their lives.

New Literacy Studies

A move to recognise learners' 'way with words' is to shift towards a literacy model based on a social approach to literacy. Social approaches to literacy are sometimes grouped together under the remit of the New Literacy Studies (NLS) (Barton, 1994; Barton and Hamilton, 1998; Gee, 1996; Street, 1984). The theory of literacy as a social practice has been strongly influenced by Street's (1995) early ethnographic research in Iran. The research findings were grounded in data that unpicked and described the many ways in which people used reading and writing for different purposes in their everyday lives. This approach which resulted in Street's theory contrasted to the autonomous and ideological models of literacy. According to Street (1996), the autonomous model of literacy 'assumes a single direction in which literacy development can be traced, and associates it with "progress", "civilization", individual literacy and social mobility ... It isolates literacy as an independent variable and then claims to be able to study its consequences. These consequences are classically represented in terms of economic "take off" or in terms of cognitive skills' and

DOI: 10.1057/9781137535115.0005

take an instrumental value position. The autonomous model then, which aligns to how most formal literacy classes are enacted, conceptualises literacy in strictly technical terms. That is, literacy is assumed to be a set of neutral, decontextualised skills that can be applied in any situation. In a nutshell then, literacy is a skill that a person either has or does not have. This concept provides a deficit framework which positions people as literate or illiterate. The autonomous model is, therefore, driven by the importance given both to individual cognition and to society through the intrinsic characteristics that literacy is assumed to have.

Conversely, the ideological model conceptualises literacy as a set of practices, not skills that are grounded in specific contexts and 'inextricably linked to cultural and power structures in society' (p.433). Within this complex view of the nature of literacy we can highlight that literacy has many purposes for the learner. It challenges the dominance of the autonomous model and recognises how literacy practices vary from one cultural and historical context to another. In the private domain of home and public domain of formal education, literacy practices, identities and discourse are produced by power and ideology so that literacy is shaped differently in different contexts.

This focus can support tutors to shift from a narrow competency-based approach, which separates the literacies from their context and instead harnesses the everyday practices learners bring into the classroom. As such literacy is not just a technical or neutral skill, it provides a social view which is expanded by treating literacy as not only a social practice but also a multi-modal form of communication. It recognises music, images, symbols and other forms as being literacy practices. The use of multi-modal literacies offers the expansion of the ways learners acquire information and understand concepts. Words, images, sound, colour, animation, video and styles of print can be combined. This approach moves from a deficit model of literacies and recognises instead that 'language, literacy and numeracy involves paying attention first and foremost to the contexts, purposes and practices in which language (spoken and written) and mathematical operations play a part' (Barton et al., 2007, p.17).

NLS offers a socially situated model which, similar to the Freirian 'culture circle', challenges dominant models of literacy. For example, it replaces the economic-driven model associated with workforce training, productivity and the notion of human capital[2] (institutional literacies) to a sociocultural model which includes vernacular literacies. In their book

DOI: 10.1057/9781137535115.0005

Local Literacies Barton and Hamilton (1998) explore the many literacy activities people are involved in across the different domains of their life. A crucial aspect of their findings is that people have 'ruling passions' which can be a key to where, why and what literacy practices mattered to them. As a tutor, knowledge of learners' 'ruling passions' offers a means to recognise and celebrate the learners' practices. Whether the practice is drawing, words, poetry or photographs like the 'Culture Circles', NLS draws on the literacies from the learners' lives. These artefacts are a way to develop a dialogue leading to an analysis of the concrete reality represented by the learners and facilitating them to address inequalities in their lives. In an Australian study Baynam (2001) illustrated through a case study the reading practices of an unemployed teenage boy in an Australian farming community and how one of his ruling passions, the weather, led him to engage in a variety of reading practices (and associated writing practices) in a variety of semiotic modes, drawing in different ways on numeracy knowledge. As such the notions of what counts as reading and the contexts where reading occurs was broadened and shaped to the teenagers' passions – an antithesis to a one-size-fits-all approach.

How can NLS be extended

Street's work points to the ideological nature of literacy, whilst Barton and Hamilton's is positioned within the social practices perspective which distinguish the ways in which literacy practices are shaped and driven by power. NLS and critical approaches to education offer a potential and rich space for transformation where learners can explore their narratives and society around them (Duckworth, 2014). However, we suggest that there are important aspects of literacy for which this model does not sufficiently offer an analytical framework. We consider a key omission to be that it does not address the real difficulties that learners may have with acquiring literacy. We propose that this can be explored by drawing sociological frameworks. Sociology of education has played a part, often implicitly, in addressing processes by which, and ways in which, schooling and school knowledge contribute to reproducing sociocultural stratification along class, ethnicity and gender lines. Some of this grew from the workings of language within the larger historical 'logic' of reproduction. Work contributing to the

DOI: 10.1057/9781137535115.0005

sociology body by Bernstein (1971, 1975) and Bourdieu and Passeron (Bourdieu, 1989; Bourdieu and Passeron, 1977) is widely known as having provided significant formative support for the sociocultural approach to literacy. Bernstein (1971) asserts that there are two language codes, restricted and elaborated. The elaborated code is aligned with the middle and upper classes and defined as a richer use of language that, for example, would utilise more adjectives whilst restricted, contrary, is viewed as more clipped and monosyllabic and aligned to the working classes. Bernstein believes that members of the working class have access to one code, whilst members of the middle class have access to both as a result of them having the opportunity to be more socially, culturally and, of course, geographically mobile throughout their life. Bourdieu argues that Bernstein fails to relate language and its codes 'to the social product to its social conditions of its production, or even as one might expect from the sociology of education, to its academic conditions' (Bourdieu, 1994, p.53). Bourdieu (1991) offers a useful tool for understanding critical theories and for seeing the ways in which critical theories bond with theories of literacy as social practice and multiliteracies. For example, Duckworth's (2013) ethnographic study drew on Bourdieu's theory to show how these ideas can offer a useful framework for analysing adult literacy learners' narratives of their lives and encounters with education. It provided a framework to explore literacy as a cultural capital and literacy education as a site of production and reproduction of power positions, where certain literacy practices are considered more legitimate than others. Indeed, literacy acts a cultural tool that provides us with capital, where capital is seen as cultural and social ways of being and doing that are represented and embodied in individuals as a habitus or part of a socially recognised credential (Bourdieu, 1991). Bourdieu's concept of cultural capital is vital in exposing the transmission of wealth and power and incorporating ideas about how those in a position of power, whom Puwar (2004) describes as 'insiders', reproduce and maintain their domination. Using Bourdieu's frame allows links to be made between language use and power against both a contemporary and historical landscape. Indeed, in unfolding the literacy learners' narratives (Duckworth, 2013), the overarching aim is to recognise and understand their narratives against the backdrop of wider socio/economic/political and historical contexts (Goodson and Sykes, 1991;

DOI: 10.1057/9781137535115.0005

Goodson, 1992). Bourdieu's fields of social, cultural and economic power overlap and feed into each other, separately and collectively offering a valuable framework for understanding the historical formation and reproduction of the research group in this study. Bourdieu's notion of habitus, with modifications, was also used to examine the historical, present and emergent character of the learners' trajectories. Juxtaposed to this, the concepts of capitals and their relationship to the learners' lives can be applied to explore their experiences of navigating through the flow (or lack of flow) of capitals in the domains they entered and the constraints, possibilities and empowerment this can offer. The learners' trajectories can also be employed to illuminate the objective and subjective dimensions of their identities and how they inform, rupture and transform the habitus in relation to the changing interplay between classed and gendered processes over the learners' life course. This, we suggest, can help to develop concepts sensitive to exploring the above, whilst examining how learners try to make sense of and deal with the challenges which they face from their structural positioning as basic skills learners.

Duckworth's study (2013, p.14) further revealed that the literacies the working-class children brought to school, and adults brought to further education, afforded little symbolic value in that it could not be used in class to pass exams. For example, the domestic and caring literacy which has been traditionally carried out by girls and women seldom enters the public domain and often remains invisible and unrecognised. The working-class practices, which were often gendered, were not valued. Wrapped in notions of literacies were domination and symbolic violence. Oral and written linguistic capabilities were not equally valued in schools (or the workplace), and even within the oral tradition, the codes of the upper classes were prioritised over the codes of the working class and ethnically diverse learners (Bernstein, 1971; Labov, 1972). This inevitably meant that learners who were not proficient in the linguistic skills required in schools and colleges were defined as failures or lacking in intelligence simply by virtue of the way they relate to and know the world.

Importantly, in the analysis and praxis of this, critical education offered Duckworth the opportunity to extend Bourdieu's concept by including this as a lever for change and the potential for learner empowerment (2013, p.14).

DOI: 10.1057/9781137535115.0005

Creativity

The move towards embedding creativity into the curriculum is often difficult, as college curricula often do not acknowledge the creativity that learners bring into the classroom. Their creativity is often masked in a process of symbolic violence where their hopes, desires and practices outside the class are not explored and instead a dominant competency-based model of literacy is delivered. Using multimodal approaches which includes poetry and images can be a move towards reflection and transformation (Duckworth and Brzeski, 2015). Shifting the habitus systems of dispositions that generate behaviours, including perceptions, expectations, beliefs and actions in a particular context, creativity can arise from sharing creativity and encouraging learners to think beyond a competency-based approach to literacy. The confidence that arises for creativity can help the learners in other fields.

Duckworth (2016) explores creativity in the form of critical and empathic imagination which can be the critical source for a pedagogy of social empathy and solidarity. The use of creative imagination as a tool for learner empowerment can be utilised by drawing on the often hidden-away practices learners bring into the classroom. For example, Duckworth (2014) identified that the cultural capital (Bourdieu, 1986) that learners brought to the classroom included the differing creative literacy practices (poetry, storytelling, monologues, song lyrics, drawing, etc.). These artefacts are a means to develop a dialogue leading to an investigation of the concrete reality represented by the learners. Multimodal approaches to teaching and learning in the educational context embraces a range of strategies that integrate a number of delivery media, which may be facilitated by the creation of information and communication technologies (Ingle and Duckworth, 2012). It was used as a means for them to engage in a variety of critical practices. Recognising students as creative agents and authors also offers an alternative vision for the future development of creativity and literacy that has the potential to improve adult educational opportunities as representational modes effecting the shaping of knowledge. It also facilitated the learners to use the cultural acts as a means to see beyond themselves and to learn to develop insights and understandings of people whose culture, ethnicity, gender and sexual orientation are different from their own.

DOI: 10.1057/9781137535115.0005

Poetry and art can be used as a way to engage learner into a critical dialogue, as illustrated in (Duckworth, 2013). An example was using Linda Lucas' (2001) poem as resource. A former literacy learner and cleaner at the college, Linda composed the poem in class during the Oldham race riots. It was based on Linda's feelings as, watching from her front doorstep, she noticed like vultures 'reporters, crew members rushed to fill their empty reels of film' to capture the images of young men fighting:

Like gladiators,
(they) Chose a weapon,
A stick, a brick, something to hurt – destroy
All sides took part – skin colour the divide.

Delivering to an ethnically diverse class, where there continued to be tensions around race and gender, the poem was used as a discussion piece which included drawing attention to the lines of the poem:

Whispers of hate threw out in despair,
Torn lives for the world to see.

The poem became a critical tool for awareness-raising from a local, national and international perspective. This facilitated the group to shape their assumptions about identity and racism. It also opened up a space to use poetry as a means for emotional expression.

Up until seeing the poem, one student had a mindset which saw reading and writing poetry as something only for those with 'qualifications and yer know good jobs'. She described how she felt scared of exploring the possibilities of language, believing it was 'not for someone like me'. Carol was experiencing symbolic violence and the:

[u]niversal adopted strategy for effectively denouncing the temptation to demean oneself is to naturalise difference, to turn it into second nature through inculcation and incorporation in the form of the habitus. (Bourdieu, 1992, p.122)

However, on reading Linda's poem she seemed totally amazed that people who lived on the same streets as her had written with so much power and emotion. She voiced: If they can do it, who are just like me, so can I.

Her position in the field changed. She soaked up the lessons, even asking for poetry. Inspired rather than running from words, she began to

DOI: 10.1057/9781137535115.0005

embrace language as something she had the right to use. She described how on shaping sentences it really helped her:

> Deal with those lousy feelings that have crammed my life too often like doubt, failure and fear.

Discovering she had a flair for writing poetry helped her realise:

> I used to think everyone was better, now I know we're all the same, equal like.

Taking control of language empowered Carol and the belief that she can use words to express herself. She turned the symbolic violence she had initially experienced into symbolic power. Carol's confidence developed together with her self-esteem.

Conclusion

The model of curriculum can determine whether education is an emancipating or suppressing process. Education institutions and government support and perpetuate ideologies that legitimate and authenticate knowledge, reproducing inequality and injustice through the practices employed (Beck, 2005; McLaren, 1988), which include the shape and implementation of the curriculum. Therefore, the lifelong curriculum, which includes Literacy, Language and Numeracy (LLN), may be situated not as neutral or apolitical but at the centre of educational power. For example, in an age of globalisation and neo-liberalism, it may be viewed as a product of market-driven changes, where approaches to LLN involve a reductive functional literacy approach. This is defined by its social purposes, in which there is an alignment between individual skills, the performance of society, the global economy and economic productivity. Easily testable outcomes, such as the LLN end tests, are often what the lifelong learning sector follows to measure performance, pull down funding and beat national benchmarks.[3] Deficits are measured against a fixed and discrete set of transferable skills. The curriculum is not static; it changes to meet the demands of a market-driven culture and as a result of the requirements of competition. What it fails to recognise and address is the historical and contemporary disparities that exist in the structural inequalities between the learners and their lives, for example, class, gender and ethnicity. It is our strong

DOI: 10.1057/9781137535115.0005

assertion that literacy is more than a set of basic skills. A social practice's understanding of adult literacy challenges the view that literacy is a decontextualised, mechanical manipulation of letters, words and figures, but is positioned within affective social, emotional and linguistic contexts. It is by challenging a skills approach to literacy development and offering a critical, co-construction model (CCCM) based on care and a social approach to literacy (Duckworth, 2014) that we can shift from a deficit perspective of adult literacy and instead engage learners in understanding everyday life situations including inequalities, which impact upon their lives. The implications of this are that the meaningful literacy practices that a community of learners bring with them, which are historically and socially constructed based on their backgrounds and experiences, are not given value in the classroom.

Literacy teachers know that teaching literacy is much more than teaching the technical skills of reading and writing. It has the potential to be a life-changing and enhancing experience for learners who are overcoming personal, social, and situational barriers to literacy learning. Therefore, the implications for practice include a recognition of the transformative experience as a part of the learning process for adults of any educational level, the importance of an authentic and trusting relationships with literacy learners in order to support this process and the potential of transformative learning to change lives irrespective of gender, ethnicity, culture and socio-economics. If we do not include analyses of the status quo, we may be reinforcing its validity. Conversely, if we do emphasise these critiques, we may be labelled as trouble makers, coercive or radical.

Practitioner research offers an empowering tool for teachers to challenge the passive position – as the recipients of knowledge – and instead generate their own knowledge (with their learners) and unsettle the status quo. In our research, Practitioner Action Research (PAR) was a key in driving practice forward, for example, rather than presuming to know what the learners want to learn and what type of resources are best; I began to listen more closely to the learners' voices, letting their needs, aspirations and dreams shape the lessons (Duckworth and Hamilton, 2016).

We strongly suggest that it is time for adult education to dis-entangle itself from neo-liberal fusion to create space for contextualised and emancipatory learning and in doing so work, 'against and beyond boundaries. It is that movement that makes education the practice of freedom' (Hooks, p.12).

DOI: 10.1057/9781137535115.0005

Notes

1   We draw on Antonio Gramsci (1891–1937), who used the term hegemony to signify the power of one social class over others, for example, the bourgeois hegemony. It embodies not only political and economic control, but also the ability of the dominant class to assign its own way of viewing the world so that those who are subordinated by it accept it as 'natural'.

2   Human capital may be viewed from a micro-perspective, for example, the way the accumulation of knowledge and skills, such as literacy practices, enables learners to increase their productivity and their earnings and macro, how this impacts on the productivity and wealth of the communities and societies they live. The dominant model of institutional literacies derives human capital from economic returns, such as employability.

3   Any discussion of LLN, and its impact in challenging the barriers and inequalities faced by many learners, cannot overlook the key issue (and what can be a real barrier) of funding. We strongly argue that LLN provision needs to be fully funded for all adults, including providing choices of flexible and accessible formal courses together with supporting those with skills at lower levels to engage in informal learning. LLN skills courses for young and older adults can offer them a crucial second chance of re-engaging with education. They can contribute to personal development, including developing soft skills such as confidence and communication, while promoting a range of economic, social and health related benefits. Along with this, LLN skills provision offers them a better chance of acquiring the tools needed to run their own lives; empowering them and their local and wider community (Duckworth, 2014b, p.20).

DOI: 10.1057/9781137535115.0005

References

Ade-Ojo, G.O. (2011) *From Symptom to Cure: The Evolution of Adult Literacy Policy and Practice in the UK from the 70s to Moser.* Hamburg: Lambert Academic Publishing.

Ade-Ojo, G.O. (2014) 'Towards a Functional Curriculum Model of Social Literacy. Literacy for Specific Purposes'. In Duckworth, V. and Ade-Ojo, G. (eds.), *Landscapes of Specific Literacies in Contemporary Society: Exploring a Social Model of Literacy.* London: Routledge Research in Education.

ALBSU. (1980) Newsletter of the Adult Literacy and Basic Skills Unit.

ALBSU. (1990) Newsletter of the Adult Literacy and Basic Skills Unit.

Allen, M. (2007) 'Learning for Labour: Specialist Diplomas and 14–19 Education'. *Forum*, 49 (3), 299–303.

Allen, M. and Ainley, P. (2007) *Education Make You Fick, Innit?* London: The Tufnell Press.

ALRA. (1976) Newsletter of the Adult Literacy Resource Agency.

ALRA. (1977) Newsletter of the Adult Literacy Resource Agency.

ALRA. (1980) Newsletter of the Adult Literacy Resource Agency.

Bailey, R. (ed.) (2011) *The Philosophy of Education, an Introduction.* London: Continuum.

Bailey, R., Barrow, R., Carr, D. and McCarthy, C. (eds.) (2013) *The Sage Handbook of Philosophy of Education.* Los Angeles, London, New Delhi, Singapore and Washington: Sage.

Ball, S.J. (1990) *Politics and Policy Making in Education*. London: Routledge.

Ball, S. J. (2003) The Teacher's Soul and the Terrors of Performativity, Journal of Education Policy, 18 (2), 215–228.

Ball, S.J. (2004) 'Participation and Progression in Education and Training 14–19: Working Draft of Ideas'. Discussion Paper for the Nuffield Review Working Day 6.

Barrow, R. (2013) 'Schools of Thought in Philosophy of Education'. In Bailey, R., Barrow, R., Carr, D. and McCarthy, C. (2013) (eds.), *The Sage Handbook of Philosophy of Education*. Los Angeles, London, New Delhi, Singapore and Washington: Sage, pp.21–23.

Barton, D. (1994) *Literacy: An Introduction to the Ecology of Written Language*. Oxford: Blackwell.

Barton, D. and Hamilton, M. (1998) *Local Literacies: Reading and Writing in One Community*. London: Routledge.

Barton, D., Hamilton, M. and Ivanic, R. (eds.) (2000) *Situated Literacies: Reading and Writing in Context*. London and New York: Routledge.

Barton, D., Ivanic, R., Appleby, Y., Hodge, R. and Tusting, K. (2006) *Relating Adults' Lives and Learning: Participation and Engagement in Different Settings*. London: NRDC.

Barton, D., Ivanic, R., Appleby, Y., Hodge, R. and Tusting, K. (2007) *Literacy, Lives and Learning*. London: Routledge.

BAS. (1973) Policy Pointer: Status: Illiterate Prospect: Zero. Newsletter of the British Association of Settlement.

BAS. (1974) Adult Literacy Campaign. Newsletter of the British Association of Settlement.

Beauregard, H. (2009) 'The Evolution of Adult Literacy Education Policy in the United States and the Erosion of Student-Empowered Learning'. A University of Ohio MA Thesis, Electronic Thesis and Dissertation Centre, Ohio.

Beck, A. (2005) 'A Place for Critical Literacy'. *Journal of Adolescent & Adult Literacy*, 48, 382–400.

Bernstein, B. (1971) *Class, Codes and Control. Theoretical Studies towards a Sociology of Language*, Vol. 1. London: Routledge and Kegan Paul.

Blattberg, C. (2015) 'Political Philosophies and Political Ideologies'. Accessed online at http://www.academia.edu/2067330/Political_Philosophies_and_Political_Ideologies on 10 May 2015.

DOI: 10.1057/9781137535115.0006

Bourdieu, P. (1986) 'The Forms of Capital'. In Richardson, J. (ed.), *Handbook of Theory and Research for the Sociology of Education. New York: Greenwood Press.*

Bourdieu, P. (1991) *Language and Symbolic Power.* Cambridge, MA: Harvard University Press.

Bourdieu, P. and Passeron, J. (1977) *Reproduction in Education, Society and Culture.* London: Sage.

Bradley, D. (1996) Who Dares Wins. Intended and Unintended Consequences of the Further Education Funding Council Methodology, Educational Management & Administration. 24 (4), 379–388.

Brookfield, S. (2003) 'Putting the Critical Back in Critical Pedagogy: A Commentary on the Path of Dissent'. *Journal of Transformative Education,* 1, 141–149.

Brooks, G. (2007) 'Assessing Adult Literacy and Numeracy: A Partial History'. *Reflect,*Issue 3, NRDC, 8 (June).

Bynner, J. and Parsons, S. (1997) *It Doesn't Get Any Better.* London: Basic Skills Agency.

Bynner, J. and Parsons, S. (2003) 'Social Participation Values and Crime'. In Ferri, E., Bynner, J. and Shepherd, P. (eds.) *Changing Britain: Changing Lives.* London: Institute of Education Press.

Bynner, J. and Parsons, S. (2005) *New Light on Literacy and Numeracy.* London: National Research and Development Centre for Adult Literacy and Numeracy.

Bynner, J., McIntosh, S., Vignoles, A., Dearden, L., Reed, H. and Van Reenan, J. (2001) *Improving Adult Basic Skills. Benefits to the Individual and to Society.* London: DFEE.

Carey, S. (2000) *Measuring Adult Literacy – The International Adult Literacy Survey in the European Context.* London: Office for National Statistics.

Coleman, J. (1988) 'Social Capital in the Creation of Human Capital'. *The American Journal of Sociology,* 94, S95–S120.

Crowley-Bainton, T. (1997) 'Encouraging Employer Investment'. Training Partnerships-Countrysides, UK.

Curren, R. (ed.) (2007) *Philosophy of Education: An Anthology.* Oxford: Blackwell.

Dae-Bong, K. (2009) Human 'Capital and Its Measurement', the 3rd OECD World Forum on 'Statistics, Knowledge and Policy'. *Charting*

DOI: 10.1057/9781137535115.0006

Progress, Building Visions, Improving Life Busan, Korea 27–30 Oct. 2009.

Degenhardt, M.A.B. (1982) *Education and the Value of Knowledge.* London: George Allen and Unwin.

DES (1977) *Education in Schools: A Consultative Document.* London: HMSO (CMND. 6869)

DFES (2001) *Schools Achieving Success.* Annesley: DFES.

DFES (2003) *21st Century Skills Realising Our Potential, Individuals, Employers, Nation.* London: HMSO.

DFES (2006) *Further Education: Raising Skills, Improving Life Chances.* London: HMSO.

Dorling, D. (2015) Why Inequalities Still Persist. Cambridge: The Polity Press.

Dradley, D. (1997) 'Influence, Compromise and Policy formulation: The Further and Higher Education Act and Adult Education'. *Studies in the Education of Adults*, 29 (2), 212–221.

Duckworth, V. (2013) *Learning Trajectories, Violence and Empowerment amongst Adult Basic Skills Learners.* Monograph. Educational Research. London: Routledge.

Duckworth, V. (2014a) 'Literacy and Transformation'. In Duckworth, V. and Ade-Ojo, G. (eds.), *Landscapes of Specific Literacies in Contemporary Society: Exploring a Social Model of Literacy.* Monograph. London: Routledge Research in Education.

Duckworth, V. (2014b) Basic Skills Provision: A Powerfultool for Challenginginequalityand Empowering Learners, Their Family and Their Local and Wider Communities,Adults Learning, NIACE, 25 (4), 19–20.

Duckworth, V. (2015) 'Literacy and Imagination.' In Bland, D. (ed.), *Imagination for Inclusion: Diverse Contexts of Educational Practice.* Monograph. London: Routledge Research in Education.

Duckworth, V. and Brzeski, A. (2015) 'Challenges to Neoliberalism: Literacy, Learning and Identity'. *Research in Post-Compulsory Education and Training*, 20 (1), 1–16.

Duckworth, V. and Hamilton, M. (2016) 'Linking Research and Practice in Adult Literacy In the UK'. In Yasukawa, K. and Black, S. (eds.), *Beyond Economic Interests: Critical Perspectives in Adult Literacy & Numeracy in a Globalised World.* Australia: Sense Publishers.

FEFC (1998) Chief Inspector's Annual Report, 1997–1998. FEFC, Coventry.

DOI: 10.1057/9781137535115.0006

FERL (2004) 'Policies and Strategies: The Foster Report'. FERL Bulletin. Accessed online at http:/ferl.qia.org.uk/display.cfm?resID=13951 on 10 October 2007.

Field, J. (1996) 'Learning for Work: Vocational Education'. In Fieldhouse, R. (ed.), *A History of Modern British Adult Education*. Leicester: NIACE.

Fieldhouse, R. and Associates (1996) *A History of Modern British Adult Education*. Leicester: NIACE.

Fitzsimons, P. (1999) 'Human Capital Theory and Education'. *Encyclopedia of Philosophy of Education*.

Foster, A. (2005) 'Realising the Potential: A Review of the Future of the F.E. Colleges'. DFES/Crown Publications.

Fowler, Z. (2005) 'History of Adult Literacy campaigns.' In Politically Constructing Adult Literacy: A Case Study of the Skills for Life Strategy for Improving Adult Literacy in England 1997–2002, PhD thesis, Institute of Education, London.

Frankena, W. (1969) 'Towards a Philosophy of the Philosophy of Education'. Reprinted in Lucas, C. (eds.), *What Is Philosophy of Education?* Toronto: Macmillan, pp.286–291.

Freire, P. (1970 [1976]) *Pedagogy of the Oppressed*. New York: Penguin Books.

Freire, P. (1993) *Pedagogy of the Oppressed*. New York: Continuum.

Fukuyama, F. (1995) *Trust: The Social Virtues and the Creation of Prosperity*. New York: Free Press.

Garnett, M. (1989) 'A Chief Education Officer of the Education Reform Act'. ALBSU.

Gee, J.P. (1992) *The Social Mind: Language, Ideology, and Social Practice*. New York: Bergin & Garvey.

Gee, J.P. (1996) *Social Linguistics and Literacies: Ideology in Discourses*, 2nd edition. London: Routledge Falmer.

Gee, J.P. (2001) 'Identity as an Analytic Lens for Research in Education'. In Segato, W.G. (ed.), *Review of Research in Education*. Washington, DC: American Educational Research Association, pp.99–125.

Gee, J.P. (2015) *Social Linguistics and Literacies: Ideology in Discourses*. London and New York: Routledge, Taylor and Francis Group.

Gee, J.P., Hull, G. and Lankshear, C. (1996) *The New Work Order: Behind the Language of the New Capitalism*. Boulder, CO: Westview Press

Giroux, H. (1997) *Pedagogy and the Politics of Hope: Theory, Culture, and Schooling*. Boulder, CO: Westview.

DOI: 10.1057/9781137535115.0006

Glaserfield, E. von. (1995) *Radical Constructivism: A Way of Knowing and Learning*. London: Falmer Press.

Glaserfield, E. von. (ed.) (2007) *Key Works in Radical Constructivism*. Rotterdam: Sense Publishers.

Goodson, I. (1992) 'Studying Teachers' Lives: An Emergent Field of Inquiry'. In Goodson, I. (ed.), *Studying Teachers' Lives*. London: Routledge, pp.1–17.

Goody, J. (ed.) (1968) *Literacy in Traditional Societies*. Cambridge: Cambridge University Press.

Goody, J. and Watt, I. (1963) 'The Consequences of Literacy'. *Comparative Studies in History and Society*, 5, 304–345.

Grek, S. (2010) 'International Organisations and the Shared Construction of Policy "Problems": Problematisation and Change in Education Governance in Europe'. *European Educational Research Journal*, 9 (3), 396–406.

Habermas, J. (1975) *Legitimation Crisis*. Boston: Beacon Press.

Halsey, A.H., Heath, A. and Ridge, J.M. (1980) *Origins and Destinations: Family, Class and Education in Modern Britain*. Oxford: Clavender Press.

Hamilton, M. (1996) 'Adult Literacy and Basic Education'. In Fieldhouse, R. (ed.), *A History of Modern Adult Education*. Leicester: NIACE.

Hamilton, M. (2005) 'A Lightning History of Learner Assessment in Adult Literacy, Numeracy and ESOL'. North West Skills for Life Forum.

Hamilton, M. (2014) 'Survey Literacies'. In V. Duckworth and G. Ade-Ojo (eds.), *Landscapes of Specific Literacies in Contemporary Society: Exploring a Social Model of Literacy*. London: Routledge Research in Education, pp.47–60.

Hamilton, M. and Merrifield, J. (2000) 'Adult Basic Education in the UK: Lessons for the US'. National Review of Literacy (1) National Centre for Study of Adult Language and Literacy.

Hamilton, M. and Hillier, Y. (2006) *Changing Faces of Adult Literacy, Language and Numeracy. A Critical History*. Stoke-on-Trent, UK, and Sterling: Trentham Books.

Hamilton, M. and Hillier, Y. (2007) 'Deliberative Policy Analysis: Adult Literacy Assessment and the Politics of Change'. *Journal of Educational Policy*, 22 (5), 573–594.

Hargreaves, A. (1994) *Changing Teachers, Changing Times*. London: Cassell.

DOI: 10.1057/9781137535115.0006

Harris, A. (1997) 'The Impossibility of a Core Curriculum'. In Philips, D. and Walford, G. (eds.), *Tracing Education Policy*. London and New York: Routledge, Taylor and Francis Group.

Havelock, E. (1963) *Preface to Plato*. Cambridge, MA: Harvard University Press.

Heath, S.B. (1982) What No Bedtime Story Means: Narrative Skills at Home and School. Language in Society, 11(1), 49–76.

Heath, S.B. (1983) *Ways with Words: Language, Life and Work in Communities and Classrooms*. Cambridge: Cambridge University Press.

Hickey, J.H. (2008) *Literacy for QTLS: Achieving the Minimum Core*. Harlow: Pearson.

Hildyard, A. and Olson, D. (1978) 'Literacy and the Specialisation of Language'. Unpublished manuscript, Ontario Institute for Studies in Education. (Referred to in Street, 1984).

Hillier, Y. (2006) *Reflective Teaching in Further and Adult Education*. London: Continuum.

Holland, C. with Frank, F. and Cooke, T. (1998) *Literacy and the New Work Order*. NIACE: England and Wales.

Hooks, Bell (1994) Teaching to Transgress: Education as the Practice of Freedom. New York: Routledge.

Ingle, S. and Duckworth, V. (2013) *Teaching and Training Vocational Learners*. London: Sage.

Joseph Rowntree Foundation (1998) 'The Roles of TECs and LECs in Regeneration'. Joseph Rowntree Foundations (Ref. No. 328).

Kwon, D. (2009) 'Human Capital and Its Measurement'. The Third OECD World Forum on 'Statistics, Knowledge and Policy' Charting Progress, Building Visions, Improving Life Busan, Korea, 27–30 October 2009. OECD. Accessed online at http://www.oecd.org/site/progresskorea/44109779.pdf on 10 February 2015.

Labov, W. (1972) *Language in the Inner City: Studies in the Black English Vernacular*. Philadelphia: University of Pennsylvania Press.

Lankshear, C. and McLaren, P. (eds.) (1993) *Critical Literacy: Politics, Praxis, and the Postmodern*. Albany, NY: State University of New York Press.

Larkin, C. (2001) Citizenship Education or Crowd Control? The Crick Report and the Role of Peace Education and Conflict Resolution in the New Citizenship Curriculum, Centre for Conflict Resolution, Department of Peace Studies, University of Bradford.

Lauder, H. (1991) 'Education Democracy and the Economy'. *British Journal of Sociology of Education*, 12 (4).

Leitch, S. (2006*) Prosperity for All in the Global Economy-World Class Skills.*HMSO, Crown Copyright, Norwich.

Limage, J.L. (1987) 'Adult Literacy Policy in Industrialised Countries'. In Arnove, R. and Graff, H. (eds.), *National Literacy Campaigns*. New York: Plenun Publishing Corporation.

Macedo, D. (1994) *Literacies of Power: What Americans Are Not Allowed to Know*. Boulder, CO: Westview.

Marples, R. (2011) 'What Is Education For?' In Bailey, R. (ed.), *The Philosophy of Education, an Introduction*. London: Continuum, pp.35–46.

Maxwell, N. (2014) *Global Philosophy: What Philosophy Ought to Be*. Imprint Academic.com.

McKenzie, J. (2001) *Changing Education. A Sociology of Education since 1994*. Harlow: Pearson Education.

McLaren, P. (1988) 'Schooling and the Postmodern Body: Critical Pedagogy and the Politics of Enfleshment'. *Boston Journal of Education*, 170, 53–83.

McLaughlin, T. (2000) 'Citizenship Education in England: The Crick Report and Beyond'. *Journal of Philosophy of Education*, 34 (4), 542–570.

Mezirow, J. (1991) *Transformative Dimensions of Adult Learning*. San Francisco: Jossey-Bass.

Mezirow, J. (1995) 'Transformation Theory of Adult Learning'. In Welton, M. (ed.), *In Defense of the Lifeworld*. Albany, NY: State University of New York Press.

Mezirow, J. (2000) *Learning as Transformation: Critical Perspectives on a Theory in Progress*. San Francisco: Jossey-Bass.

Moore, G.E. (1960) *Principia Ethica*. Originally published 1903. Cambridge: Cambridge University Press.

Moorhouse, C. (1983) 'The Right to Read Re-visited'. *Media in Education and Development*, California: Thousand Oaks Publication, pp.144–145.

Neufville, R. (2014) 'Instrumentalism'. In Bevir, M. (ed.), *Encyclopaedia of Political Theory*. Thousand Oaks, CA: Sage, pp.702–703.

OECD (1998) 'The OECD Employment Outlook-Towards an Employment-Centred Social Policy'. *The OECD Observer*, 213 (August/September).

DOI: 10.1057/9781137535115.0006

O'Keefe, D. (1999) 'Political Correctness and Public Finance', IEA, Harrington Fine Arts Ltd, Lancing, West Sussex.

Osler, A. (2000) 'The Crick Report: Difference Equality and Racial Justice'. *Curriculum Journal*, 11 (1) (March), 25–37.

Parsons, S. and Bynner, J. (1998) *Influences on Adult Basic Skills*. London: The Basic Skills Agency.

Parsons, S. and Bynner, J. (2002) *Basic Skills and Social Exclusion*. London: The Basic Skills Agency.

Parsons, S. and Bynner, J. (2005) *Measuring Basic Skills for Longitudinal Study: The Design and Development of Instruments for Use with Cohort Members in the Age 34 Follow-Up in the 1970 British Cohort Study (BCS70)*. London: National Research and Development Centre for Adult Literacy and Numeracy.

Paterson, R.K.W. (1979) 'Towards an Axiology of Knowledge'. *Journal of Philosophy of Education*, 13, 91–100.

Payne, J. (1990) 'Recent Trends in Central-Local Government Relations'. Local and Central Government Research Programme Report 3: PSI.

Phillips, D. (ed.) (2000) 'Constructivism in Education: Opinions and Second Opinions on Controversial Issues'. *99th Yearbook of NSSE*. Chicago: University of Chicago Press.

Phillips, D. (2007) 'The Good, the Bad and the Ugly: The Many Faces of Constructivism'. Reprinted in Curren, R. (ed.) (2007) *Philosophy of Education: An Anthology*. Oxford: Blackwell, pp.398–409.

Phillips, D. (2013) 'What Is Philosophy of Education?' In Bailey, R., Barrow, R., Carr, D. and McCarthy, C. (eds.), *The Sage Handbook of Philosophy of Education*. Los Angeles, London: Sage Publications, pp.3–20.

Phillips, D. and Walford, G. (eds.) (2006) *Tracing Education Policy*. London and New York: Routledge, Taylor and Francis Group.

Powell, J.L. and Edwards, M. (2005) 'Surveillance and Morality: Revisiting the Education Reform Act (1988) in the UK'. *Surveillance and Society*, 3 (1), 96–106.

Pring, R. (2004) 'The Skills Revolution'. *Oxford Review of Education*, 30 (1), 105–116.

Pring, R. (2005) 'Labour Government Policy 14–19'. In Philips, D. and Walford, G. (eds.), *Tracing Education Policy*. London and New York: Routledge, Taylor and Francis Group.

DOI: 10.1057/9781137535115.0006

Pykett, J. (2007) 'Making Citizens Governable? The Crick Report as Governmental Technology'. *Journal of Education Policy*, 22 (3) (May), 301–319.

QCA (1998) 'Education for Citizenship and the Teaching of Democracy in Schools'. Final Report of the Advisory Group on Citizenship. London: QCA.

Randeep, Ramesh (2015) http://www.theguardian.com/politics/2015/may/08/tories-conservatives-12bn-welfare-cuts

Reay, D. (2005) 'Beyond Consciousness? The Psychic Landscape of Class?' *Sociology*, 395, 911–928.

Reay, D., David, M.E. and Ball, S. (2005) Degrees of Choice: Social Class, Race and Gender in Higher Education. Stoke-on-Trent: Trentham Books.

Rikowski, G. (2006) 'The Long Moan of History: Employers on School Leavers'. *The Volumizer*. Accessed online at http/journals.aol.co.uk/rikowskigr/volumizer/entries/1182 on 25 June 2007.

Robinson (1983) The Users and Uses of Literacy. In Richard W. Bailey and R M. Fosheirn, (eds.), Literacy for Life: The Demand for Reading and Writing. New York: The Modern Language Association of America.

Rosseau, J.J. (1955) Emile, (trans.) Barbara Foxley. London: J.M. Dent and sons Ltd.

Russell, Sir, L. (1973) *Adult Education: A Plan for Development*. DES: HMSO.

Sayer, R.A. (2011) *Why Things Matter to People: Social Science, Values and Ethical Life*. Cambridge: Cambridge University Press.

Scottish Executive (2001) Adult Literacy in Scotland: Analysis of Data from the 1996 Adult Literacy Survey. Edinburgh: Scottish Executive.

Sellar, S. and Lingard, B. (2013) 'PISA and the Expanding Role of the OECD in Global Educational Governance'. In Meyer, H.D. and Benavot, A. (eds.), *PISA, Power and Policy: The Emergence of Global Educational Governance*. Oxford: Symposium, pp. 185–206.

Shor, I. (1992) *Empowering Education: Critical Teaching for Social Change*. Chicago: University of Chicago Press.

Silver, R. (2007) 'Learning Works: Ten Years On'. University of Greenwich Education Research and Enterprise Newsletter, 10 (Autumn 1).

Skinner, R. (1972) *Beyond Freedom and Dignity*. London: Jonathan Cape.

Small, R. (2005) *Max and Education*. Aldershot: Ashgate.

DOI: 10.1057/9781137535115.0006

Standish, P. (2011) 'What Is the Philosophy of Education?' In Bailey, R. (ed.), *The Philosophy of Education, an Introduction*. London: Continuum, pp.4–19.

Street, B. (1984) *Literacy in Theory and Practice*. Cambridge: Cambridge University Press.

Street, B. (1995) *Social Literacies: Critical Approaches to Literacy in Development, Ethnography and Education*. London: Longman.

Street, B. (2001) 'The New Literacy Studies.' In Ellen Cushman, Eugene R. Kintgen, Barry M. Kroll, and Mike Rose (eds.), Literacy: A Critical Sourcebook. Boston: Bedford, pp.430–442. Print

Tomlinson, S. (2001) *Education in a Post-Welfare Society*. Buckingham: Open University press.

Torrance, H. (2002) 'Can Testing Really Raise Educational Standards?' A professorial lecture delivered at the Institute of Education, Manchester Metropolitan University, UK. Accessed online at http://www.enquirylearning.net/issues/education/HTassess.html on 9 July 2007.

Torrance H. (2003) 'Big Change Question: As National Policymakers Seek to Find Solutions to National Education Issues, Do International Comparisons Such as TIMMS and PISA Create Wider Understanding, or Do They Serve to Promote the Orthodoxies of International Agencies?' Invited contribution to discussion symposium in Journal of Educational Change, 4, 419–425.

Tucket, A. (2001) 'If I Can't Dance ... Convivality and Adult Learners'. Lecture delivered at the University of East London as NIACE chairman, January 2001.

Vygotsky, L.S. (1979) *Thought and Language*. Cambridge, MA: MIT Press; see also http://www.learningandteaching.info/learning/referenc. htm#ixzz3btyqtHdg Under Creative Commons License: Attribution Non-Commercial No Derivatives.

Winch, C. (2000) 'The Education Reform Act'. *Labour and Trade Union Review*, November 2000

Wordsense.EU Dictionary (2015) Accessed online at http://www.wordsense.eu/ on 12 February 2015.

DOI: 10.1057/9781137535115.0006

Name Index

DOI: 10.1057/9781137535115.0007

DOI: 10.1057/9781137535115.0007

Subject Index

DOI: 10.1057/9781137535115.0008

DOI: 10.1057/9781137535115.0008

DOI: 10.1057/9781137535115.0008

DOI: 10.1057/9781137535115.0008

DOI: 10.1057/9781137535115.0008

CPI Antony Rowe
Chippenham, UK
2018-01-22 21:40